```
F
.K13   Kaniuk, Yoram.
          The story of Aunt
       Shlomzion the great.
```

Temple Israel Library
2324 Emerson Avenue South
Minneapolis, MN. 55405

Please sign your name and telephone number on the above card.
Books and materials are loaned for a period of three weeks and may be returned to the Library or Temple reception desk.
Fines will be charged for any damage or loss of materials.

THE STORY OF

AUNT SHLOMZION THE GREAT

Also By Yoram Kaniuk

Rockinghorse
Adam Resurrected
The Acrophile
Himmo, King of Jerusalem

The Story of
AUNT SHLOMZION
The Great

Yoram Kaniuk

**Translated from the Hebrew
by Zeva Shapiro**

HARPER & ROW, PUBLISHERS
New York, Hagerstown, San Francisco, London

This work was first published in Israel.

THE STORY OF AUNT SHLOMZION THE GREAT. English translation copyright © 1978 by Harper & Row, Publishers, Inc. All rights reserved. Printed in the United States of America. No part of this book may be used or reproduced in any manner whatsoever without written permission except in the case of brief quotations embodied in critical articles and reviews. For information address Harper & Row, Publishers, Inc., 10 East 53rd Street, New York, N.Y. 10022. Published simultaneously in Canada by Fitzhenry & Whiteside Limited, Toronto.

FIRST EDITION

Designed by Eve Kirch

Library of Congress Cataloging in Publication Data

Kaniuk, Yoram.
   The story of Aunt Shlomzion the great.
   Translation of ha-Sipur-al dodah Shelomtsiyon ha-gedolah.
   I. Title
PZ4.K165St 1978   [PJ5054.K326] 892.4'3'6   78-2066
ISBN 0-06-012259-5

78 79 80 81 82 10 9 8 7 6 5 4 3 2 1

1

The day Uncle Nehemiah died was hot; even the old-timers whose recall reached back to Baron Rothschild's stay in Rishon insisted they had never seen its like. The crowd, arriving from diverse places in cars and buses that sent up a dense trail of dust, merged with beggars who rattled money tins; their slow gestures seemed transfixed. Nehemiah's cronies, remembering the favors of their youth together, arrived in bright summer suits and ties, dimly transparent, suggesting the conceit of souls embodied in flesh. They walked the gleaming gravel path hoping to grasp their own desperate longing for themselves. Elegant white-haired ladies in bold broad-brimmed summer hats, moving timorously, slipped coins into the beggars' boxes. Appearing to be made of seared earth and champagne, they advanced toward shelter in measured pace, as if floating through the heat.

Aunt Shlomzion the Great could be seen at a distance, wearing a splendid black dress—beautiful as a raven. Old Mrs. Virsovsky, who had been sewing for Aunt Shlomzion the Great for forty years now, hobbled toward me, drew a pale pink handkerchief from her purse, wiped her nose and said in a voice smooth and crystallike: Even the tears are melting, Aminadav. What a waste . . . we're like fragments cut out of a scrapbook; the features are blurred. See what's left of us, of our entire glorious generation. Our tears melt in the heat.

Beggars cried in hollow voices: Charity redeems from death, charity redeems from death; tired birds circled the sky, then disappeared. A body was carried from the mortuary followed by men and women in black whose wails filled the blazing square. Aunt Shlomzion the Great, in all her splendor, stood watching the wailing women with filtered fury. She turned to Little Mother Shlomzion: That man of theirs could have waited till tomorrow to die. Those dark people are so pushy. We'll never have a decent culture!

Mrs. Virsovsky sighed and said to me: Isn't she beautiful in the dress I made? She came for three fittings in the last few weeks. Before she dies, she'll go to the cemetery and lie on the ground to measure out her grave. She likes things whole but she takes people apart and breaks them. She is so hard to fit; she came again and again until the dress was just right. She has such a difficult body.

The people crowded together in the shade of the flowering fig tree near a broken bench and looked toward Shlomzion the Great. I think that Mrs. Virsovsky, the Polish seamstress from *Salon Gay Paris,* intended to suggest, while considering in her own mind who should stay and who should go, that Aunt Shlomzion had prepared with great deliberation for this moment. There was a trace of irritation, or was it idolatry, in her voice. She was one of the few women, other than Little Mother Shlomzion, who remained on speaking terms with Aunt Shlomzion the Great. The Kapilowitzes, huddled together, pale and overdressed in clothes that had been in the closet for twenty years, were saying: She seems triumphant in the midst of pain; she understands death . . . our Shlomzion.

As soon as the wailing women were gone, Shlomzion turned toward the band of cantors crowded together in their black coats drinking cold soda water in the shade of a creeper. She didn't bargain at all. For the first time in her life she agreed to pay the price. They, in turn, would pray for Uncle Nehemiah. Twenty lirot worth of prayer. Not ten, not fifteen . . . Fervent prayers with God's name properly articulated. They all went to the mortuary and, following a signal from Shlomzion, moved toward the grave. The heat was oppressive, rock-heavy. Not a single drop of sweat could be seen on Shlomzion's brow. She glanced toward the remains of her beloved, to whom she had been married forty-two years less one month, a marriage of unspeakable bliss, and, for the moment, seemed bathed in a rush of light despite the trappings of sorrow. Looking out beyond her fixed eyelids, she sized up the crowd; looking out beyond Nehemiah's body, she arranged the crowd, piling layers of hate on one another. Counting heads, she focused on the absent, discounting children. She counted all of old Tel Aviv, subtracting the dead with vehemence, indifferent as she realized that old Shmulovitz, dead and buried nearby, was indeed unable to attend. Still, he was not altogether excused. She kept track of those absent though not dead, and each one of these she buried within herself with specific enmity, weighing her own beauty fearlessly and without compromise or doubt. That ravenlike beauty, so suited to the elegant dress, was pitched against the weary travail of those who withered in the heat before her eyes. The cantor prayed in a twenty-lirot voice, and two distinguished elders, venerable men who had known Nehemiah in his youth, offered a few words.

Fierce longing stood in the air. Men of distinction met themselves, the children they once were. Treetops sank to the ground. Roots soared upward, sweeping the people, vigorously, toward a time when there was iron in the air and hope. A thin man in an open shirt, unknown to those assembled there, spoke of Nehemiah's position in science, in its avant-garde. Everyone wondered—who was this man? A potential heir . . . or did Aunt Shlomzion give the University a vast sum, getting this speech in return?

He seemed detached from these ancient people, probably unable to grasp their infinite dejection. Nehemiah, he said, was endowed with that mix of curiosity and unrelenting innocence that produces artists, saints, scientists and great sinners. He spoke of chromosomes and the fungus of life. Shlomzion the Great wasn't listening. I stood watching that scarred and fragile tribe and noted that Ketzia, having stopped crying, was wiping sweat from her brow and moving quietly toward her husband's grave. She held a wreath in her hand and seemed to flutter between the two graves. From the distance Aunt Shlomzion regarded Ketzia with open hostility. Once more the birds were circling overhead, and all about was bracing silence filled with death and menacing. The hot air stood over us, dense and bitter. A plane skimmed the sky, slowly, breaking the silence for but an instant; then, once more, it was in total command. The aircraft cast a yellow shadow. Lights, rather beams, like swords, pierced the air. Dr. Genichovitz said: Poor Shlomzion. Nehemiah is gone now. They are going at a dizzying rate. It's a punishment, to come here so often and leave behind the beautiful children we once were—tired now, in the cold ground. He spoke to Nehemiah now and Aunt Shlomzion stared at him in amazement, for he was not required to speak; still he spoke . . . speaking from deep inside, for all those present, now huddled together, clinging to each other, yearning for sudden intimacy. He said: Dear Nehemiah, I told you once —we are the desert generation. Now see what we wanted, what we dreamed, what actually occurred! What were our dreams made of that we have become so unworthy of them? You, Nehemiah, did beautiful things; even loved. Did we forgive you? Did we understand you? Were we at your side for the difficult moments? I am familiar with many dreams, with many of the dead. How many live ones do I still know?

Aunt Shlomzion the Great loomed like an ornate reproach. I thought: She is still considering whether or not to let me say *kaddish*. Her son was not there. She had waited until a quarter to four. All of the flights had arrived from New York. She had spent the night in the airport. In his cable he had said he would try to come. She refused to show us the cable. I suppose he stammered even in the cable. My cousin was afraid to come. Still she wouldn't allow the likes of me to say *kaddish*. She had told Little Mother Shlomzion: If he's so anxious to say *kaddish*, let him say it for his own father. Mother had said: But Naftali is alive! Aunt Shlomzion the Great responded: Alive, but for how long? Aminadav's *kaddish* is right for Naftali, but not for Nehemiah. Nehemiah deserves a *kaddish* fit for a king, but for his sake I would make do with that despicable son of mine, who didn't bother to turn up and will regret it the rest of his life. She was jubilant for a moment, then recovered the measured mournful demeanor that so suited her.

Aunt Shlomit said: She even chose the weather! She wanted to watch all this suffering. They began to leave, eyes salty from tears and heat. Ketzia was still standing beside her husband's grave, pulling petals from a wilted red flower. This translucent old woman was muttering to her dead mate: Loves me, loves me not, loves me, loves me not. It was probably the last and only time I saw Aunt Shlomzion almost kneel. She was watching Ketzia, engulfed in her ancient private light, and approached as if about to embrace her. Then she turned to us and scolded: Who love? What love? Nehemiah isn't here anymore, and who could love Ketzia anyway?

She moved slowly, leaning on Mother and on me. The Kapilowitzes said: What love! Her splendid image seemed, for the moment, to blur, even crumble, so that I said: Aunt Shlomzion, I am sorry, I am really sorry. She looked back to the void of the cemetery, where the lost years were heaped on one another, row upon row of human shards now treading over Nehemiah's grave, stealing another moment from him stubbornly. She noticed neither the transparent pain in their eyes nor the longing. She saw her enemies and said: They are alive but he had to die. Then she wiped a tear that appeared for that particular moment and vanished, adding: They care? They don't care about anything. Do they care for Nehemiah? They thought the weather would be good, that there would be a celebration and I would forgive them. How many flowers did they bring? Old flowers, from other graves. Didn't Adonsky himself die covered with flowers from all of Tel Aviv's cemeteries?

We didn't answer, neither Little Mother Shlomzion nor I. She climbed into Amihud Milqwite's car, yelling: They will laugh now, with all their gadgetry, gorgeous houses bought on my account. But Nehemiah will stay here. And she drove off.

They watched her go, a troupe of aged children, each seeking refuge, but running singly—pale, weary, driven by heat—toward cars, cabs, bus. The square was empty.

Seven days of mourning followed. Hardly speaking, we looked at Nehemiah's photographs and medals. Mother served coffee brought from her own house. Aunt Shlomzion the Great said they were unworthy of coffee from her kitchen. She sat in her room; from time to time she would bring out old photographs of Uncle Nehemiah and Adonsky, her father, evidence of their absolute beauty.

2

She was called Shlomzion the Great because she was four years older than Mother Shlomzion. Little Mother Shlomzion, who was Nehemiah's sister, was somewhat shorter than Aunt Shlomzion the Great. Nehemiah died in September, 1961. He was sixty-five when he died.

Aunt Shlomzion the Great is now ensconced in the only private hospital in Tel Aviv, in a room that costs about twelve thousand lirot a month. Those who regard themselves as her heirs are aligned, each in his separate corner, as their hopes shatter and dreams grow dim, smiling at one another—polite glassy smiles—phoning Little Mother Shlomzion or the hospital with dwindling patience and indifferent voices, straining to conceal their frantic lust, seeking to confirm the day of Aunt Shlomzion's death.

Every morning, as if by chance, one of these unfortunate heirs arrives at one of the banks to check into Auntie's financial situation. They drop into a branch of any of several banks in town, failing, again and again, to receive a reassuring answer. The complexities of her financial network are so involved and intricate that no one—outside of Auntie herself, whose mind is slowly calcifying—knows precisely how much money she has now, how much she had and how much will remain. The funds are invested in bonds, securities, savings accounts, short-term loans linked to the dollar. Those who seem to know contend that vast sums are tied up in mysterious currencies.

Seasoned lawyers, most of them old-timers who remember Shlomzion from their youth, call each other and carry on long casual conversations in pleasant voices that conceal a tremor. They try to clarify their positions, to find out whether they, in fact, represent Shlomzion the Great, whether they remain responsible for some portion of her estate or were perhaps never actually entrusted with it. In their ancient offices, lined with shelves full of dusty law tomes, and overshadowed by old diplomas, portraits of Ben-Gurion and British High Commissioners, photographs of historic handshakes, they sit trying to trip each other up with clever strategies. Their hair is white, their faces wrinkled and rosy. As they confer together, their hands tremble, their eyes stray past the empty windows onto the deserted streets. Their lives have been wiped out. Nothing is as it was. The young sharp-witted lawyers sit in new offices on other streets. The old-timers have been bypassed, remaining no more than fleeting shadows, a striking contrast to aggressive sons in handsome sports cars . . . they who so wished to preserve some of the daring vitality of their young days, filled with Shlomzion and Adonsky, with the fierce and enthralling battle over my cousin's name.

Aunt Shlomzion knew many lawyers. Throughout her life she hired lawyers, going from one to another, meeting furtively with bold young attorneys who, by now, have also aged, issuing secret directives, mysterious instructions leading to blind alleys. She wrote five contradictory wills, placed them in safes whose combination was disclosed, in part, to a pair of lawyers unknown to her own lawyers, the major and significant link being known to an elderly justice of the peace who, for some years now, has been in the hospital for the chronically ill in Raanana, a gentleman who happened, long ago, in his youth, to be strolling through Jaffa's citrus groves picking flowers in time to see Shlomzion returning from the shore after the French ship fired five shells at the factory of Wagner, the German—Shlomzion having just attained a state of ultimate exhilaration.

I thought: I will decipher the code! Imagine Shlomzion's dismay. The judge would wonder, too: Aminadav? Of all people! As long as he is able to wonder. Days pass. He is destined to die. The heirs don't know. He thinks: She was happy then; it was almost sixty years ago. Shlomzion is such a beautiful girl! He still dries rare flowers. Shelves full of flowers . . . No one to bequeath them to, so they crumble. Alone in a wheelchair, smiling; so many codes. So many contradictions. What a powerful woman she is! And copies of the letters—only some of which are clear, the others baffling, to become clear when the fragments can be joined, those that were left with Little Mother Shlomzion as well as those in the hands of the brother in Chicago! Not to mention her unknown agents, plowing through the night, greeting the morrow with a new round of instructions!

Shlomzion does not regret the price (twelve thousand lirot a month) of her room. Life filters through to her neutralized by a prism of hate. She sees my mother's soft face, anxious nurses, trees, a window and the roofs of houses built on land belonging to Adonsky, her father, land sold at an exorbitant price.

Disappointed in life as she had almost lived it, Aunt Shlomzion the Great was seduced by the relative certainty of a hospital environment. She is seventy-six now and insists, even when there is no reason to insist, that the doctor is in love with her. In her words: That attractive and clever young man is head over heels in love with me. Aunt Shlomit gets daily reports from one of the nurses and says, in terms characteristic of anyone who has tried being close to Aunt Shlomzion the Great, that Auntie couldn't possibly see the doctor's heels because (a) she doesn't see very well, (b) young doctors are not barefoot when examining old women.

The doctor is forty-two years old. His gray hair is stylishly cut. At the moment she is inclined toward the clean-cut, sterile, even somewhat sweet look. The doctor appears to her to be of good family, not of the marginal sort who excel in their studies and become doctors. There are several things she simply does not tolerate: nervous young men possessed by violent passions, reforming the world, fulfilling their destinies. She likes people to be smooth. She dislikes, rejects . . . even this is inaccurate. She approves or accepts this doctor—that's it. But I have almost been ensnared in other people's webs. Though my subject is Shlomzion the Great; who is so unique.

Every day this handsome well-bred doctor examines Shlomzion the Great an extra time (beyond the routine). He is paid in dollars by Shlomzion's brother in Chicago, who is required, by the terms of directives transmitted to him through a noted lawyer and certified by a celebrated notary, to make available whatever sum is requested. This document further specifies: Nor will you have the right to an opinion in these matters; you will be informed of a reward for your services at the appropriate time through this or some other channel, as well as of my concern for you.

She is unwilling to communicate with her brother. She was considered Adonsky's only child, her brother's birth being an indiscretion unworthy of note. In 1917 her brother abandoned the Land of Israel and went to America despite her pleas, an act she never forgave. She was a young girl then and had come to him declaring: If you go, I will never speak to you again! He laughed at his little sister's folly, kissed her on the cheek and left.

She has not spoken to him since, neither when she visited the United States nor when he visited her country.

At Uncle Nehemiah's funeral her brother felt for the first time in his life what it is like to see yet not be seen.

He is an old man now, almost eighty. When he realized the extent, in dollars, of the sum she had entrusted to a famous Boston lawyer (some of which was accessible to him solely for the aforementioned payments), he rushed a letter to her, filled with emotion and nostalgia. He wished, after nearly sixty years, that they could come to terms . . . so he wrote; for was not the end approaching and what was there beyond the deep and tangled ties of family and blood, common memories known only to the two of them, and the heritage of their great father?

She answered (with the lawyer as intermediary) that she was indeed aware of the source of his extreme and superfluous, not to mention unaesthetic, sentiments. Moreover, if he felt he was on the brink of death he ought to appoint a younger man to take over the payments. She, for one, did not intend to die. She was living in a hospital now, a secure enough place. The memories to which he refers are of no interest to her; they provide no common ground. One must be willing to live in this land to be worthy of sharing memories. She does not intend to forgive his treachery and warns him against using her father's name in vain —for she might have an attack of chronic amnesia when writing her will.

3

Aunt Shlomzion arrived at the hospital about a year ago. One day she felt she was going to die. It was a Wednesday, she told me, and old Nahumi, the teacher, passing her house as he did on Wednesdays, just by chance, dropped in to ask if he could look at Nehemiah's stamp albums. Nahumi, who used to teach Aunt Shlomzion the Great folk dancing and patriotic songs, was by now bent almost to the ground. She answered, as always, that she could not allow stamps to be stolen every Wednesday. Nahumi doesn't give up, she told Little Mother Shlomzion. For ten years now, perhaps longer, he has come regularly on Wednesdays, unless he is sick or something, asking to see the stamps. Why does he come? And why should I allow it? He has his eye on the triangular stamps from Portugal. I told Shlomzion that those stamps were not so valuable, that there were more valuable stamps in the collection. All that glitters is not gold and not every triangle is treasure, I said. She glared at me. I quickly added that I knew this to be a fact because, as she herself was well aware, Uncle Nehemiah had showed me his marvelous collection many times. Ever since, she said dryly, fifteen stamps have been missing. They were probably worth 150 sterling. As usual, I didn't respond to her charges. I explained that I myself did not believe Nahumi intended to steal stamps. Only then did I add what she was waiting to hear: Stamps are of no interest to him. He is half blind; what could he see? He has been in love with you since 1912. His only wish is to have tea with you and to drink in your beauty with his half-dead eyes.

Aunt Shlomzion said haughtily: These dirty old men! You think it's tea he's after? He'll push me into bed and make a child, the idiot!

Aunt Shlomit once dared to suggest that at seventy-six women rarely become pregnant. To this day she regrets the remark.

That particular Wednesday, after old Nahumi was out of sight, Aunt Shlomzion the Great sat in her huge empty house gazing, without compassion and without forgiveness, at the many furnishings that once knew Uncle Nehemiah's touch, at the books he had read or written. Alone she sat, enclosed by a sheaf of light from the tiny ceiling fixture (having replaced all the lights with smaller fixtures, to conserve, as she termed it, my dwindling resources), doing as she had done most of her life—nothing. Aunt Shlomzion the Great sat at the window of her desolate room, midst fine pictures framed in gold, old bookshelves, diplomas and medals, stamp albums, old pegs on which Nehemiah's hats and official suits still hung. . . . She sat and hated. The phone was silent, the windows locked. Still, all at once, Death appeared and stood before her, so tangible. She gazed at him wishing to say he had come to the wrong address. Her body ached, her heart began pounding rapidly. She felt faint, as though moving through a heavy fog, sinking into bottomless depths.

She always had, and still has, beautiful eyes—black set in hollows of purple. Her hair is white but flowing, her skin is fresh and tight, her body unbent, her breasts full and shapely. Her fine skin has a vague flush, suggesting the decline of matter. But this is offset by a slim firm body. In the words of Aunt Shlomit—who watches Aunt Shlomzion the Great with a brand of pleasure mixed with envy and pain such as only a woman approaching seventy can conceive for one of seventy-six who looks sleek, pretty, fresh, endowed with female wiles, yet seasoned—she is nature's wonder, preserved and enriched, ripe and mellow as old wine.

Can anyone fail to be struck by Aunt Shlomzion's solid and singular beauty? Only Aunt Shlomit has dared to say, speaking through some forty years of suffering, that evil, obsessed and in love with itself (Aunt Shlomzion, for example), living a lifetime on stage under garish spotlights, is the negation of all negative qualities and, as such, constitutes a unique challenge to the deterioration of flesh and the ravages of time. Aunt Shlomit said: She ages less like wine than like vinegar. Aunt Shlomit is preoccupied with fermentation. She reads whatever she can find on the subject and her conversation refers repeatedly to the fermentation and preservation of substances. She is a small woman. Her husband, Abner, is dead. Shlomzion the Great has banished her. Longingly, she loves the old clock bequeathed by her father, a clock which tells time as it sees fit, and has no need to repair it. She sits on her balcony reading about fermentation, caressing the memory of the sea which could once be viewed from that spot . . . before the new houses were built. She is an expert on the wines of Rishon-le-Zion and Zichron Yaakov; the balcony is crowded with tubes full of greenish muck and rancid fluids. She says we were all once amoebae.

She wouldn't say that, Little Mother Shlomzion remarks, had she not been buried alive by Aunt Shlomzion the Great. Such is the fate of those who seek Auntie in vain.

See what she does to us, to all of us, Little Mother Shlomzion says sadly.

From behind the mounting fog Aunt Shlomzion the Great observed Death penetrating her sealed fortress. She had placed double bolts on all her doors, sealed the windows with the most sophisticated devices! But the awareness that no lock can withstand Death made her mistrust conventional barriers. Remembering her great moment when that young French officer came ashore, just before the five shells were fired by the ship in the direction of the factory of Wagner, the German, she told herself: No one can be trusted!

She sat immobile, youth aged and contained in a box. An exemplary woman. She watched Death climb the fig tree, leap onto the branches of the bougainvillaea and from there to the top of the four-story house next door. She wanted to scold him, to say that even Nahumi, her poor troubadour, doesn't scale walls for her: he pretends to be interested in stamps. A little finesse, my dear! It wouldn't hurt, she thought, her body groaning with the pain of matter crumbling proudly even while seeking amends, searching for kindness. The house across the way, a handsome four-story structure, its front (unseen from Aunt Shlomzion's courtyard) constructed like a cardboard model of a Greek temple, once had a very different identity. Why doesn't he find a victim there?

But they were all gone, all the Marxes, Neventhals, Katzes. Gone. This place was something then . . . when Dr. Lev lived there with three pedigreed hounds and "Hello, Frau Shlomzion! . . . *Wie geht's,* Frau Shlomzion." They've all gone. And now? The big house is teeming with small publishers, promising lawyers, secretaries in short skirts typing triplicate letters to nonexistent clients, with comic vitality. The courtyard is neglected, littered with trash; the shrubs and trees grow wild and cats fill these disenchanted days with insolent howls of psychosomatic love. She was overwhelmed by faintness and felt sad (a feeling which was unfamiliar, so much so that she didn't realize she was sad) about houses abandoned without reason, once splendid courtyards filled with secretaries in short dresses typing letters in triplicate to people whose addresses they cannot verify, ugly rooms decorated with landscape paintings and old calendars, publishers of small art books to be sold at kiosks that once offered fruit juice, nectar, chilled citrus and lemonade. Death continued to climb the bougainvillaea, and the humiliation that swept over her was more warning than pain. So Aunt Shlomzion the Great called the hospital and said: Shlomzion speaking. Please send an ambulance; it's urgent.

The doctor on duty, drinking tea and watching the TV movie,

asked who she was, where she lived, father's name, her age, medical coverage, the nature of her problem. She was offended, nearly forgetting Death. She scolded the doctor, who seemed indifferent but gracious even after her harsh and bitter tirade. She said: Maybe it was you, personally, who sent me Death. Like in America when I was there. Traveling salesmen go from door to door telling people they're sick; they extort money and disappear. Then doctors come selling drugs. They come in the same car, she said.

The doctor watched the rest of the old Western in silence. A woman shrieked in the wooden hut. The sheriff galloped toward a misty wasteland.

Send an ambulance. Quickly. Listen, she said, even before your father was born, Adonsky, whose only child I am, built the cities in which you will raise your ugly unborn grandchildren.

The doctor laughed. The sheriff arrived at the little wooden hut and the girl was overjoyed. The masked culprit hid behind the door. The train robbery was daring enough, but still the doctor knew justice would triumph, a somewhat disheartening fact. Genuine laughter, of the sort that is expressed with sound and smile, was as foreign to Aunt Shlomzion as the desperate shape of deep sorrow. No one laughed in her presence. The doctor's laughter seemed like a rare tropical flower. She could not fathom it.

She said: You make strange noises. I hope I didn't call the zoo by mistake. And slammed the receiver.

The doctor came in person.

She knew he would.

She had put on a relatively new dress in his honor, and arranged her hair. She ordered him to take her to the private hospital in north Tel Aviv. She was not about to share a room with groaning patients, weeping women, other people's bedpans. She has been living there ever since, though she recovered long ago. She pays twelve thousand lirot a month, not counting an extra fee for the visits of the stylish gray-haired doctor. She sent the doctor on duty a box of chocolates received from an elderly lawyer who visited her the day after she was hospitalized. She wanted to wrap it in newspaper, but Little Mother Shlomzion explained that old newspaper would be regarded as a misunderstanding rather than an attempt to offend.

Imagine, said Shlomzion the Great, that fellow was sitting there in the Tel Aviv hospital not knowing my name. He wanted to know my father's name. . . . Those scoundrels have ruined everything that was good and beautiful.

All her life Aunt Shlomzion the Great has been standing at her own finish line, fishing for herself, longingly, in the depths of a mirror framed in gold. She loves herself in technicolor; she hates the world in black-and-white.

One of the children Aunt Shlomzion calls "monkeys, born like stray cats, they will surely die of some street disease," once told me the beautiful old woman could be God in disguise. He had in mind her intensity, extending to Nahumi, who appeared at her doorstep at regular intervals to be oppressed; to Aunt Shlomit, who came and went whence she came; to passersby, who looked longingly at the handsome clothes worn by aged lawyers in taxis, arriving at her house in an agitated sweat, only to return shortly thereafter, flushed and mumbling to themselves. He didn't know what lands were owned by her father, nor did he know the marvelous chronicles of her family. Still, Shlomzion always was a propelling force in his world.

He was a bright kid. I don't remember his name. (He wasn't expecting an inheritance.) Once, he told me, he brought Aunt Shlomzion milk from the store. After searching through her pockets, which were full of coins, she found a penny which she gave him as a tip. He didn't know how she happened to have pennies. He said that she had smiled angelically when she gave him the penny. The trees didn't bow to her, he said. He didn't throw the penny in her face, nor did he say thank you. He simply left. She, undoubtedly, assumed he was fresh like his parents. Though she didn't know them, she could tell from his face who they were and what they were worth. At the time of this incident Aunt Shlomzion had the flu. Little Mother Shlomzion was in

Jerusalem that day, caught in a snowstorm. Nahumi came only on Wednesdays. Apart from these two, she had no callers other than Aunt Shlomit, who used to wait near the house for a moment, lost, and leave without going in. Aunt Shlomit never rang, having been cast out even before she arrived. So there was no one to get the milk.

The heirs call her on the phone. They are waiting tensely for the day of her death. Her life is of no interest to them. It should be noted that they don't know if they are truly heirs, or merely delude themselves. Little Mother Shlomzion and I have decided we are not heirs. We told her so. On this occasion we were all in agreement. When I told Little Mother Shlomzion what Aunt Shlomzion the Great had said about the boy, and what he had said about her, she was angry. She couldn't be God in disguise, she said. Little Mother Shlomzion associates God with goodness, suffering, sacrifice, life force, generosity, grace: the antithesis of evil. Such innocence!

Nonetheless, I detected in Little Mother Shlomzion's face an inexplicable love for the old woman who had cursed and tormented her all her life. I thought: Because Little Mother Shlomzion believes beauty is pure and evil crystallized, she can, maybe, love Aunt Shlomzion the Great. Whatever is pure and crystallized enchants her, fills her with awe and sympathy. I defended the child's theory. It was the eve of Shabbat. Little Mother Shlomzion and I were in a small seaside café in Tel Aviv overlooking the water. The sun was about to sink into a calm sea. Little Mother Shlomzion comes here to remember the old casino, to recall the old days when she was voted Purim Queen. We watched the waves lick the shore. I said: Look here, she destroyed her son. His life is ruined, he stutters, his marriage is wrecked, his children wander through the world seeking forgiveness without knowing why. She abused her husband, Nehemiah, made everyone miserable. What can one say for her? Remember Nehemiah's final days?

Little Mother Shlomzion was silent. She drank her coffee, captivated by the infinite beauty of the sea. She may have been seeing herself, a lovely young girl running across the sand in a long skirt, pursued by two mustached youths . . . a carriage headed for Jaffa moving down the road . . . a small group, meticulously dressed, going down to the sea to greet the Shabbat. A scene of arresting yet contained charm. I said: Poor Nehemiah, he lay there half dead, swollen, the doctors saying he would die in a day or two. He was heavily sedated, his mind was hazy. Only his beautiful eyes remained prominent, as if peering out of a dim cave. He tried to smile. Remember. And she wouldn't let him eat *leben!*

Mother Shlomzion's face darkened. She put down her coffee and turned away from the scenes of her youth forgotten in sands now crowded with whores, hippies, soldiers and fishermen.

She tightened her lips, opened her eyes wide and pounded on the table. She spoke with excitement resounding with anger I could not comprehend: You don't understand, Aminadav. She loved him. She loved three people in her life: her father, a grandfather she never knew and Nehemiah. She loved Nehemiah with pity, rage, cruelty, madness. Throughout her life she was dedicated to a single cause: loving Nehemiah and preventing anyone else from touching him. He was a brilliant scientist, right? He knew all about cancer. Still he pretended to believe the doctors when they said it was a severe ulcer. He pretended and she played the game to protect him from people like you who knew he was about to die and thought a glass of *leben* could hardly hurt a man who is about to die. But, clutching a straw, he believed the doctors. He needed Shlomzion to forbid him to have *leben*, so he could delude himself! It seems terrible to you, as if she was sparing the *leben*, but it was an act of love, Ami, awesome love. Do you think, cruel as she is, that she would deprive him? He sought hope in every sign and this was a sign. Like your entire generation, you don't understand love, my mother said, watching the sea turn darker and darker.

Look, I said, after a while, you may be right. But he was already so incoherent that a little *leben* could have only brought him pleasure before . . . Remember—all that time, just before he died, when we were all sitting at his bedside, she was staring at me to be sure I didn't steal stamps. She went from room to room checking everyone's behavior, seeing that no one took books, stamps, a cup, a knife from her old service. Her beloved is on his deathbed and she is obsessed with the triangular stamps from Portugal!

Too bad you didn't take the stamps, Mother said suddenly. Her face, so tender until that moment, turned hard and bitter, a consequence of fifty years with Shlomzion the Great. She moved toward the railing at the edge of the walk, glanced out at the sea, returned to me, repeating: Too bad you didn't take the stamps! Why does she sit on all those millions? She could do so much. ... But she loved him.... There was no room for us. I loved him through her net for fifty years.

Little Mother Shlomzion began to cry, special tears stored up over the years for that moment, and said: Those stamps belonged to Grandpa. We all collected stamps for Nehemiah after he inherited the collection. That collection doesn't belong to her; it belongs to you. You are the true heir. You resemble your grandfather; you are his closest blood relation. But she won't give it up. The bitch ... Then Mother was silent. She sat, wiping a tear, and said: But you are wrong about the *leben.*

4

Over the years her circle of friends, dependent on her idiosyncrasies, frightened by her insults, diminished steadily. Many had died or were slowly dying; some succumbed to despair. A few lonely widows were left in the area, as well as two old spinsters, all of whom related to Shlomzion with dwindling indulgence, a token of their loyalty to common childhood memories. As for her, she spared no one. Still, Little Mother Shlomzion is right: she has charm, mystery, beguiling brightness, crude nonverbal wit. Perhaps it is we who were to blame, Mother Shlomzion and I, for not grasping, for being unable to grasp, solid irrevocable hate, pure envy, groundless yet absolute. The compulsion to act in terms of consistent unrelenting evil is alien to us. We are people who can be won with a smile, a tender word. It may be just this quality that makes Little Mother Shlomzion aware of the anguished and mysterious love suppressed by Shlomzion the Great throughout her life.

One day I went to the bank to co-sign some papers for poor Johnny, who had to remortgage his apartment when his three ex-wives and his current girl friend, who was having a hysterical pregnancy, confronted him all at once with unreasonable demands. Absorbed in thought and concern for my friend and the consequences of his stormy love life, I had parked illegally and stopped at a nearby kiosk for some soda. The day was hot. The soda looked murky and tasted of rust. Beyond the trees I spied the splendid house of Aunt Shlomzion the Great, with its ornate tower barely visible through a sea of cars, buildings converted into offices, a rushing mass of people pressed by time. I went back to the car to get the papers and found a ticket. A sweet policewoman grinned at me from a distance.

I called to her: Look here, I was gone for a minute. She retorted: What's done can't be undone, honey. I enjoyed her neat aphorism, said thank you and went into the bank occupied with visions of policewomen sweet as traffic signals on a lollipop stick. On the way in I met Aunt Shlomzion the Great. This occurred about a year before she took sick.

In her pale blue dress and large straw hat, Shlomzion looked like a Gainsborough portrait. She said: Ami, what are you doing here? Give your old aunt a kiss. She offered her face with the precision of a trained traffic cop, leaving me no choice but to kiss the moist powdered cheek. She stared at me an interminable moment. I didn't know what to say. In the distance her house looked bereaved and sorrowful, its pointed roof like a clown's hat. I don't know why I thought of that image. Her eyes were searching and I felt guilty without knowing the source of my guilt or why, in her presence, I always feel like a guilty clown. I said, without being asked: I'm here to sign Johnny's papers.

Ah? Shlomzion doesn't hear well, and shouts, like all deaf people who resist hearing aids.

Johnny . . . Noam Haimson; Yigal's son.

Your mother won't come herself? Aunt Shlomzion the Great asked. (The policewoman was circling my car, jauntily. Was she planning to give me another ticket?) She sent you to spy on me? Let me tell you something, Ami. What I have here, in this bank, is only a fraction of what I possess. Which is another thing you'll never know.

I came to sign some papers, Auntie, I said.
Of course, she said in a tone that drowned out the roaring traffic. The policewoman looked alarmed.
I came to rob the bank, I offered feebly. Maybe she'll believe me at last.
She didn't laugh. She didn't know how to laugh—like Adonsky, her father. Nor did she acknowledge the sound of laughter.
She said: Rob the bank or sign!
Deciding to behave gallantly, I offered my hand, put my arm around her and in we marched together.
She said: Arpahshad, the rat! My good-for-nothing son! What does he write you? He wants to know if there will be anything left for him? Not a fig. Let him find salvation in America, anti-Semitism, mixed marriages and all.
I told her I hadn't had a letter from him since 1950. Calculating quickly, I remarked: Twenty-four years, Aunt Shlomzion. That's a long time.
He writes and writes to everyone, she said. Only not to me. And if he did write what could he say? I warned him not to marry that whore. Now he has four wild children and a wife who works in a brothel.
She is doing very well at the Massachusetts Institute of Technology, I offered. And one letter in twenty-four years is not exactly an impressive correspondence.
He talks to everyone, she said, about me and me again! But it won't help him. He is stupid and corrupt, the worst thing that ever happened to me. Now your mother and my son are conspiring, trying to trap me, to put me away in an old people's home with toothless hags, and cannibals. Listen, Ami, your role is very minor; you don't even understand why they send you to spy on me. If my son isn't behind this absurd comedy, then my name isn't Shlomzion.
I didn't say a word. Better be a spy on her son's behalf than try to prove anything to her. We moved on, studied by many baffled eyes only too familiar with the woman in blue. I watched the teller's

face pale as we stood in line. He fixed his eyes on Shlomzion the Great. She said: Aminadav is here to sign some papers; so he says.

That's right, I agreed.

Papers? The teller, who was as wrinkled as old parchment, did not hear me and screamed: Papers! There was a moment of silence in the huge bank. All eyes turned on him. He blushed, began fingering some documents, then wiped the sweat from his brow. Straining to understand what Shlomzion had said, he began muttering: What, how, why, where, when.

His friend's papers, Aunt Shlomzion exclaimed in her resounding voice.

Johnny's papers, I said. Noam Haimson.

What?

Poor Noam Haimson, I repeated.

Ahah! A deep sigh of relief. He was saved. The bank resumed its former tempo. The papers are here, he's certain. What is she doing in this young man's company? The teller was revived.

I signed the papers that were handed to me with a trembling hand.

She studied me throughout.

Your hands are shaking, Ami. You ought to see a doctor. Not your mother's cheap doctors—they're all thieves. Go to Dr. Levin. He's the only one I trust.

I gave the teller the papers, put my pen in my pocket and smiled. She had put me in touch with reality again. I said to her: Aunt Shlomzion, Dr. Levin died two years ago. I came to take you to the funeral, and you told me you were sick and a dead doctor's diagnosis is no better than a live one's, not that Dr. Levin ever gave a worthwhile diagnosis even when he was alive. So you said.

And I went?

No, you didn't go.

Those scoundrels die off, one after another, she said—not angry, not glad, with the indifference of a tour guide. It's the lawyers who don't die, she decreed. Old Nahumi and the lawyers will live on forever. Why did he die, Ami? Why did he have to die? I know already. I yelled at him for a whole hour because of the useless drops he gave me. He had a heart attack and died.

That was much earlier, I said. He died on a trip, in the company of a young woman. He died like a man.

I was always struck by her apathetic gaze, its cold incisive edge. I added: Don't you remember?

She was silent. Then she began screaming again: Remember? I stopped seeing him in '55. The faker. To my son's friends he was vaguely male. To me he was simply a bore, a fat body occupying too much space in the world. He prescribed aspirin for sunstroke. They're all fakers, Ami. He gives candy and aspirin; he has a big dog and a smooth tongue. Did you sign already?

Yes, I said.

Your hands were shaking, Ami. That's what your mother does to you. You can spy from now until doomsday, but you won't learn any more than you now know.

We stood there, neither one giving an inch. She yelled, then I yelled. We were standing in front of the bank, creating quite a stir. Passersby snickered and stopped to listen. The bank clerks glared at us with restrained hostility and suspicion. She was disappointed that I hadn't come to spy on her.

Why don't you go to the other banks with your mother and find out how much I managed to save though you all robbed me and left me with only a few pennies to my name?

Because it doesn't interest me, nor does it interest my mother. What?

Your money, Aunt Shlomzion.

She considered this and might have allowed a smile to grace her lips . . . if only she knew how to smile.

Why doesn't it interest you? You think you'll get something without any effort?

I told her words she never expected to hear. I said: I don't think I deserve anything, Aunt Shlomzion.

She pondered my words for a moment. Something inside her was provoked, incensed, offended. But she didn't show it. Aunt Shlomzion isn't stupid. The words are always poised, on the tip of her tongue. What I had said was incomprehensible and therefore alien and menacing. She was fascinated by the tone of the words, their quality. Meting out her feelings carefully, she retorted: You're trying to ingratiate yourself, to buy the favors of an elderly aunt with Communist tactics!

Aunt Shlomzion, I said, I have to go.

Yes, she said. There's never time to visit an old aunt.

I'll come, I said.

Listen, the account here is only a small part. She was shouting at the top of her lungs. I have accounts all over the country . . . and the world. She uttered the word *world* in a sudden whisper.

Again, the bank held its breath. And how is your mother? She hasn't been looking well. And your boys?

The girls are fine, I said.

So charming. But why should they suffer? I have an acquaintance in Switzerland, a good Jew. There is a surplus of men there. They have a candy factory and money and ancient castles. They're looking for Israeli brides. . . . Your poor girls could find husbands there and bring them back home. Here, poor things, with faces like theirs, it won't be easy. Our boys die in the wars and there aren't enough to go around.

Thanks, I said.

The older one, she asked, was she left back again?

They put her back two grades, I said. Next they'll move her to the zoo. They're not sure what species she is, but they're working on the question.

She scrutinized me carefully and said: Don't tease your poor aunt, Ami. I don't intend to write a new will, but I would like to help your daughters. If you find this hard to take, you can forget it. Looks aren't everything. What counts is that they stay here, in our country. Look at this city. It's going to pieces. Everyone here is sick. Someone stopped me on the street to ask directions. What do they take me for? An information center? There was a time when they wouldn't dare, but the riffraff is taking over and where can we go? Take care, Ami.

I kissed her and went on my way. She returned to the bank to check if I had misled her. I think she knew I hadn't misled her. She wanted me to think she was unsure. She always has to have the last word.

5

Aunt Shlomit, who had been trying intermittently, for twenty years, to maintain relations with Shlomzion the Great, as is the custom in families, drowned her utter failure in a cup of Turkish coffee. It was a rainy, dismal night when I decided to call on her. She said to me: That woman spreads poison! The one thing she has to offer is poison! Aunt Shlomit fell silent, observing me through webs of melancholy spun in the course of twenty-eight years of single-minded obstinacy, webs through which she viewed the world, alone and obsessed with her interest in fermentation. She added: But she will not be forgotten. Virtue is forgotten, but not evil, Ami. Who is more likely to be remembered, my husband, Abner, or Adonsky, that scoundrel! Shlomzion's father is remembered far more often than your excellent grandfather. Adonsky's funeral was the grandest in Tel Aviv's entire history—a vast crowd, weeping, wailing, bearing flowers, stood on a long line that wound its way to the grave. Did you notice how many bouquets there were? An enormous garden was denuded to cover the fresh grave. Who is she? Adonsky in a skirt.

I am fond of Shlomit. Her husband, Uncle Abner, was my friend.

Every week or two we drink coffee together, superb coffee which she personally roasts, grinds and prepares, following the old Bedouin tradition. Then she shows me the test tubes and reads me selections from the latest research on fermentation and decay. After these preliminaries we are candid with each other. I said to her: Aunt Shlomit, you of course know who came to Adonsky's funeral!

She smiled and sipped some coffee, dredging up a rush of memories and frozen sadness. She said: I know nothing. A huge crowd turned out! That's all I know. That's all I need to know. There were barely one hundred people at Uncle Abner's funeral. Who remembers him now outside of you and your mother?

Adonsky's death was an unforgettable event. Shortly before his death he composed an addendum to his will, which he sent to his lawyer Mahluf Abu-Ayid in Acre, intending to teach the citizens of our town a lesson. Mahluf, the lawyer, hired five hundred Arabs at the rate of 3.5 grush apiece, plus expenses. They were brought to an abandoned house in Jaffa in the dead of night, given clothes bought at the flea market, skullcaps and all, and instructed not to speak to anyone at the funeral the following day. There was even a rehearsal at which the Arabs stood in a circle around Hawaja Mahluf, moaning and wailing in such great distress that they themselves were speechless.

Mahluf hired an entire kindergarten, teachers included, and provided each child with the branch of a tree. An entire school from an isolated village in the north was transported in trucks at night; these children displayed an oversize map with the lands bought by Adonsky in the course of his long lifetime marked in prominent relief.

On the day of the funeral, when eight of the town dignitaries arrived at three-thirty at the old cemetery on Rehov Trumpeldor to meet with the family of the deceased, the atmosphere was tense. The elders had come deeming it only proper that there be official representation at the funeral, which was sure to be poorly attended. Seven of the eight dreaded the impact of Aunt Shlomzion's lashing tongue.

Then the crowd began to stream toward the gate of the cemetery: the school, teachers included, the entire kindergarten, as well as five hundred Arabs bearing wreaths. The night before, bouquets had been collected from all the cemeteries in the Greater Tel Aviv area, so that each Arab would carry a bouquet and Mahluf would nonetheless reap a significant profit over and above the (small) sum allotted by Adonsky. Local chieftains supervised their flocks, appearing for all purposes to be Jews and wailing with wondrous devotion, having loved Adonsky with all their hearts.

Shlomzion the Great looked joyful in black.

Little Mother Shlomzion was astonished.

Words have wings, and in twenty minutes the broad square teemed with people running to see the huge funeral. The dead man had attracted a crowd of twelve hundred in half an hour.

Reporters for the leading newspapers did not succeed in interviewing the mourners. So deep was the grief that those in the funeral procession were at a loss for words. The mayor, arriving at the last minute, buttoning his jacket all the way to the grave, delivered a moving speech. He spoke with emotion, having just realized that Adonsky had many friends and that his own political future was perhaps not as secure as he had presumed. Having neglected to prepare a speech, he repeated words offered some weeks earlier at the funeral of another one of the city's founding fathers, an enterprising and widely loved man.

Adonsky, he said, was a cornerstone. From a vale of tears to a gate of hope; acting and reacting; serving and deserving. A man whose deeds are not dead. For virtue never *ends,* but *extends.*
. . . Note the play of letters, the splendid economy of our language: the letters *het-yud* spelling life *(hai),* signifying the number 18 and also denoting a basic prayer which is not merely a melancholy series of blessings but a signification of hope. Eighteen is youth, the future, the promise of the crimson thread. He spoke at great length. The Arabs wailed. Reporters began search-

ing for hats as religious functionaries stared irately at their bare heads. Aunt Shlomzion stood proud beside her father's grave. I was counting the grains of sand under my left foot.

Mr. Avrahami spoke, too. The impromptu speakers began to vie with each other. The cantor intoned in a grand mellifluous voice and the bus drivers on Rehov Trumpeldor brought their vehicles to a halt in final tribute to someone they knew nothing about. People spoke about the event for many days. They said: Did you see how many friends he had? Could it be that we were mistaken? The surprise was overwhelming; it included an element of profound disappointment. Perhaps envy. That man knew how to die just as he knew how to live, departing from our city as he had arrived in it, with a grand gesture. He was ninety years old when he died. The vision of his funeral is still engraved in my heart. Children in white bearing branches in their arms. An entire school presenting its bold map of the country. Songs about Trumpeldor, the one-armed hero, and about Adonsky. Arabs wailing at the graveside. A long line of strangers assembled on the loose earth. Dismayed expressions. Aunt Shlomzion's aristocratic manner. The sea of flowers. White shirts, skullcaps, tears, astonished dignitaries unable to comprehend that which unfolded before their eyes. Was it a display of chivalry or unimagined love?

For some reason Aunt Shlomzion the Great divulged the secret to me. One day, as she sat in her garden hating the flowers, the grass and the sky, I happened to pass her house and caught sight of her in the yard, extravagantly dressed and full of glorified hate. She looked at me somewhat distractedly, studying me for an instant as if I were a dividend chart or a bank receipt. When she recovered her sense of reality and realized who I was, she swung her arm as if to brush away an offending fly. She said: So it's only you, Ami, the buddy of my idiot son.

I sat on the grass, enjoying its contact with my body. It was a pleasant summer day, not too hot. She said: You saw the funeral he made himself? Was my son there? No, he wasn't. He won't come to his father's funeral either. Nehemiah is in Haifa today. You don't drink tea!

No.

I don't have coffee, she said. There's juice in the refrigerator but don't take it. I'm having important guests for dinner. If you're really thirsty, there's water. Take some.

I'm not thirsty, I told her. She relaxed and her eyes began to wander again.

Do you know what Adonsky did, she said? He organized it all. I know, even though he didn't tell me. He was overcome by a surge of compassion and a lust for vengeance. He was such a beautiful man. They don't begin to measure up to him. They forget quickly. They won't forget me, don't worry!

I'm not worried, I said.

I told Aunt Shlomit the story more than once. There were still some people who didn't know the secret. Aunt Shlomit is devoted to fermentation and suffering and, like the rest of us, it pleases her to focus on her own sorry lot . . . Abner's neglect, his meager funeral.

The scoundrels sink into the ground, she said, but the fine souls, the good and pure ones, hover in space.

Once again she is returning from a protracted voyage, a twenty-eight-year struggle with a woman who has been subjecting her to systematic oppression. For twenty-eight years Aunt Shlomit has been coming "to chat," "to drink tea." Still Aunt Shlomzion the Great persists: Tell me, Ami, has Shlomit married Abner yet?

Aunt Shlomit weeps into clasped hands. Aunt Shlomzion, I reply like a broken record, they were married on the eighth of May, 1936, at the beginning of the riots. You don't remember? It was a dim night. Abner had just come back from the Jaffa-Tel Aviv border. Avigdor Bohovsky's brother was killed. We could hear the shooting on Allenby Street. The wounded lay outside the school. Abner arrived in knickerbockers, his pants stained with blood, carrying a Mauser with a wooden butt. You wore black to the wedding and said that Chopin was a relative on your mother's side. When Aunt Shlomit kissed you, you asked who she was.

Yes, I remember, says Aunt Shlomzion the Great, on the brink of laughter. (But for the fact that she can't laugh.) Who is she? Who is she anyway?

Let her speak directly to me! Aunt Shlomit declares.

What is she saying? Aunt Shlomzion the Great asks.

She says you should speak to her directly.

Who is saying I should speak to her directly? Aunt Shlomzion asks, her face registering honest dismay and innocence. Who is she? She's not from the family. Not that I'm so thrilled with the family. Many mongoloids have made their way into our blood—on Nehemiah's side, of course. Why is she inviting me? Who is she anyway?

She says you danced at her wedding, I repeat. Good Lord, Aunt Shlomzion, it all happened over thirty years ago. You danced! Uncle Abner waltzed with you and you wanted to crush the glass.

She is a dreadful woman, Aunt Shlomit says in the presence of Aunt Shlomzion the Great whose face remains innocent. . . . She turns to her: Have you no pity, Shlomzion! Poor Abner died six years ago. After twenty-six years of marriage. Why, why . . . ?

Everyone is marrying nowadays, says Shlomzion. What do they know? What for? To fill the world with mongoloids? You tell me, Ami. You appear to be a sensible fellow, though not very civilized. When Shlomit decides to marry Abner, as is proper and prescribed, you can tell her for me—

Here I am! Tell her I'm here, that I want tea, that I want company. I'm tired of test tubes and fermentation.

You can tell her I'll give her the little rug she loves when that day comes, Aunt Shlomzion exclaims.

I'll tell her, I say.

There were of course some rational grounds for this confusion. I should explain. Aunt Shlomzion the Great is not mad. If she were mad, all would be simpler. I, for my part, contend that she is more normal than anyone, but there are grave differences on this subject and I would rather avoid heavy family polemic.

When Aunt Shlomzion makes a statement, one must trace her logic, not ours, follow her connections, not ours. She sees the world as she decided it will be, because she is comfortable with it. For example, in the matter of Aunt Shlomit, who weeps on her shoulder and begs to be admitted to the family: "The gate is sealed, my sister-bride."

Aunt Shlomzion is adept at striking an enemy's vulnerable spot. Her world consists of Nehemiah and Adonsky as against the enemy camp. Uncle Abner, before making Shlomit his wife, was married to Masha, who died in childbirth when Deena, my cousin, was born.

Masha was in a frenzied state when she bore Deena. Her own mother had died in childbirth. My cousin Deena, who dreaded what she labeled "the dying mother's fate," was determined to marry the first man she could, to love him, if possible, and to have a child. To live or die. She couldn't live on the brink of terror. Shlomit had been Deena's teacher. Deena brought Shlomit home because she knew that if Abner would love Shlomit and marry her, she, Deena, could concern herself totally with her own affairs.

Shlomit and Abner did, in fact, fall in love with each other. My cousin was attuned to her teacher's soul as well as the soul of her father. She created their marriage, found herself a mate, married at a young age, proceeded to become pregnant and wait tensely.

The family was riddled with fear, everyone except Uncle Abner, a declared atheist who scoffed at superstition. He scorned those who knock on wood, a practice derived from tapping the cross, for here we are engaged in building a new nation, building and being built, and there is no place for primitive beliefs and old-country rites in our new and constantly renewing country.

Everyone pitied him, knowing that in eight months his daughter would die.

He sneered at them, laughed a lot, drank wine with Deena on Saturday nights, sat on the porch playing chess games that never ended. He went to the casino as often as he could. Danced the fox trot. Invented a new toothpaste. Believed only what could be grasped in his hand. Tested through intelligence. He was rational to an extreme degree, a Jewish atheist: one who believes fervently that he doesn't believe.

Even on the way to the hospital he ridiculed the fatalists. There is no such thing as an inherited curse, he insisted, and no danger if a cat crosses your path. I am a Zionist, a believer in national revival, he told Deena.

Her belly was bloated with the baby and she focused on approaching death.

Only when Deena was admitted to the labor room did Abner become totally distraught. He tried frantically to block the birth with his own body. He shrieked: Don't let her give birth! He wept and was led to another room where he continued to sob. Overnight his dark hair turned gray and his youthful face was covered with wrinkles. In those hours, while we all sat waiting for my cousin to die, Abner aged thirty years.

The baby was stillborn. My cousin left her husband and embarked on a new life. Uncle Abner remained sad and dejected, retaining a sense of reproach and unfathomable bewilderment. Aunt Shlomzion the Great believed in his marriage to Masha. She believed in this marriage as a death knot and she knew all about death knots. Once a month she goes to the cemetery and enacts the marriage ceremony. She stands over Nehemiah's grave, talks to him and declaims: I am betrothed to you. She lies on the loose sand of the adjacent plot reserved for her, closes her eyes tight, extends her hands and feels herself united with her husband in a sly and generous eternity. When Deena brought forth her dead baby, Shlomzion the Great announced: Abner let her die because he wanted to marry the greenhorn.

Aunt Shlomit came to the country in 1909, at the age of two, but Shlomzion continued to regard her as a new immigrant throughout her life. Abner shouldn't have allowed his daughter to marry, Shlomzion the Great contends. She proceeded to spread rumors that Masha didn't die but commited suicide over Abner's affair with the greenhorn. The fact that Aunt Shlomit was still a baby when Abner married Masha was irrelevant. Then

Shlomzion the Great extended her animosity to Deena. She refused to acknowledge her marriage and claimed that Deena, with her own hands, had killed the most beautiful baby in the family—the one, she said, who most resembled Nehemiah. When, in a moment of conceit, my mother, Little Shlomzion, suggests that I resemble Nehemiah, Shlomzion the Great responds with astonishment and pity for poor Mother: But, Little One, Nehemiah was handsome.

Deena, so says Aunt Shlomzion the Great, wanted her beautiful baby to die. She wanted Arpahshad to be Nehemiah's sole memorial. Deena is a sinful girl, Shlomzion the Great asserts, and Abner and Shlomit were her accomplices.

6

In her bright room in the private hospital in north Tel Aviv, Aunt Shlomzion the Great preens, honoring her enmity. She prefers remaining in the hospital, though there is no need for her to stay there. She hires private nurses who quit at the rate of one a week, and pays twelve thousand lirot a month, plus a significant sum in dollars to the stylish gray-haired doctor. Some say her advancing senility is paralleled by an increase in evil nature.

I like to come to the hospital. Her devotion to her own looks excites me. She weaves her demons into great and glorious fairy tales. I am not a potential heir, so I am unaffected by Shlomzion's extravagance. I won't even inherit the stamp albums. Watching her nurse her beauty, I consider how often cold precise beauty conceals the flaws in things (or people). She grooms herself intently, with zealous devotion, changes her dress every day; her hair is combed perfectly. She receives no visitors. Only Little Mother Shlomzion and I come and, occasionally, two or three lawyers. The doctors tiptoe past her room. She primps for herself alone. This is what fascinates me. She wouldn't waste an old robe on either Mother or me. Her beauty is destined solely for her own intoxication, requiring no audience. She plucks her eyebrows, massages her face, does her hair twice a day, looks in the mirror often. She is so aristocratic with her silky gray hair and smooth complexion!

Under the window, overlooking a yard filled with geraniums and roses, stands a simple white chest adorned by two photographs. Her son's picture was discarded long ago. Only Nehemiah and Master Adonsky, her two beloveds, remain. The few people who happen by tend to inquire: What about Arpahshad?

They say this for the sheer pleasure of mouthing the name, nothing more. Then they seem to mock her, to be grappling with her merciless and unrelenting shame. One of the doctors asked me: Why not Ham, like Ham son of Noah? Or Kedarlaomer? Or Tiglas-Pileser? They had forgotten the battle over my cousin's name or, more likely, were pretending. Aunt Shlomzion the Great had engaged in the battle of her lifetime over that issue, fighting for the very right to be Shlomzion. Thereafter she allowed Nehemiah to be her master for the rest of his life. The birth of her second son (the first, a mongoloid, died at the age of one year) granted her a singular opportunity to put them all in their place, to establish once and for all that her submission to Nehemiah, submission founded on great love, was of her own choosing. She chose to make him her master not out of duty or obedience but as the outcome of a struggle. It was, indeed, her goal to be defeated in the long run, but in terms of the immediate, she strove to make everyone acknowledge her right and power. Aunt Shlomzion calls this personal choice.

When my cousin was born, everyone anticipated another disaster, being wondrously well versed in the tangles of the Adonsky family tree. And what was not known could always be invented. The origins of this man were, after all, a mystery and mystery breeds a proliferation of envy and distortion. Shlomzion's family was said to have a strong strain of madness, going back to the time of our ancestor Nahor. Everyone was familiar with the tale of Ben-Amram, Shlomzion's legendary grandfather on her mother's side, an emissary from the Holy City of Hebron who traveled through Europe and Asia only to disappear with funds collected on behalf of Hebron's synagogues. Stories about Ben-Amram's Grandfather Reuven—a prominent Frankist who led a rabbi's wife through the town on a horse, naked, set fire to a synagogue, set forth to bring salvation only to be devoured by dogs—were exchanged in the four Holy Cities early in the last century. There were several versions: Reuven himself had Messianic pretensions or, in another tale, was a follower of Yosef de la Reine, who went as far as God's throne, beyond the mountains of darkness, where he captured Lilith and Satan but succumbed to their pleas and provided them incense to drink, a fatal transgression which enabled Lilith and Satan to free themselves and obstruct redemption. Other shocking transgressions were reported. And there was talk of family fathers performing ascetic rites naked in the Safed snow, or in the nettles in summer, walking through the woods and returning, their faces incandescent, going north to Sidon and even as far as the Queen of Greece, who did not know it was they who took her every night only to return to Sidon in the morning. When her first child was born, Aunt Shlomzion the Great attributed the mongoloid strain to Nehemiah's blood, since his family had so much insanity and many corrupt individuals like my Grandfather Simha. His fault, in her eyes as well as in the eyes of her father, was that he had once bought a lot (on the corner of Allenby and Rothschild Boulevard) for a bishlik, so he could tether his donkey which he used to ride to the girls' school at Neveh-Tzedek; later, when he no longer needed the donkey, he sold the lot for that single bishlik. Anyone who sells a lot for the price he paid, so she reasoned, brings mongoloid children into the world. But why judge her? She was overwhelmed with her sorrow and forgot all the madness in the Ben-Amram family, on her grandfather's side.

At birth my cousin was a darling baby weighing almost four kilos. His head was covered with downy black hair. His face was expressive. In the delivery room Aunt Shlomzion said to Nehemiah: He's so handsome, our little Wondrous-Counsel-Prince of Peace. Nehemiah replied: Over my dead body! He will be called Simha, for my father, may he rest in peace, and for the joy *(simha)* of having a firstborn male child. This was the error of his lifetime.

Shlomzion consulted Adonsky, her father, and her father said: Simha? Name him after that fool? First of all, he died in a garret. Secondly, he sold a lot for a bishlik, and that is criminal. A man who is unwilling to profit or to let another Jew profit is inhuman. Land, after all, is the only thing of real worth, and it is no longer being made. He wasn't aware that Mark Twain had said this before him. But Mark Twain did stop in the Land of Israel, and the two could actually have met. And so when my uncle decreed that his son was to be called Simha while Shlomzion decreed that he would be called Wondrous-Counsel-Prince of Peace, the curtain rose on a drama that is recalled to this day by genteel old ladies, transparent in their musty, overfurnished parlors, in tones suggesting a mighty cosmic prank that occurred generations back, before the Flood or at the time of the Tower of Babel, a grim prank, resplendent with jest, the sheen of time, the patina of fate and eternity.

My son will be called Simha, my uncle proclaimed with rare conviction, and Aunt Shlomzion was silent. There was no point in arguing. She already knew then what the compromise would be.

She had time.

She was, as always, poised for battle.

A week later, when she came home from Freund Hospital and said: Nehemiah, Wondrous-Counsel-Prince of Peace cried through the night, my uncle, for the first time in his life, slammed the door and shouted from the other side: I won't sign! No son of mine will be called Wondrous-Counsel-Prince of Peace! And he strutted off to the dunes, which were already called the boulevard.

The conflict between Nehemiah and Shlomzion began to acquire the character of war. There were screaming bouts, doors were slammed vigorously, charges hurled in both directions, countless nights when Nehemiah slept in the dunes while Aunt Shlomzion remained in the fortress with "her cub," shouting out the window: I won't give in, you might as well know it!

After a few days the noisy warfare came to a standstill, abrupt as its beginning. The new strategy was one of quiet animosity mixed with venomous despair. The street fights from the boulevard to the window concluded with the locking of the window. The rage was contained in drawers. Shlomzion consulted her father, Adonsky, who, being sick at the time, was beginning to feel an odd intimacy with the birds in the yard and, for the first time in his life, to confront metaphysical concepts such as the small step from birth to death.

Adonsky advised his daughter (this became clear later on) to forgo the name Wondrous-Counsel-Prince of Peace in principle (which she had planned to do anyway); not to inform Nehemiah of this turn; to resist any attempt to name the newborn Simha, after that bearded Zionist zealot who sold a lot for a bishlik, that pathetic poet who may have danced with the nymphets in Gay Paree and proceeded to die in a garret poor as a church mouse —and to wait patiently.

Aunt Shlomzion heeded her father's advice.

And so began the second round. Shlomzion ensconced herself in her room, locked her husband out and for a year and a half my cousin was referred to as "that one." Again and again, Nehemiah walked the sparse streets of the new city. People who once loved him were sorry for him and nodded sympathetically. In this small city of twenty thousand souls, including eleven dentists and fifteen salesmen of matches, it was not easy to be the nameless child of parents busy slinging arrows at each other—though they loved each other desperately.

Shlomzion was in constant communication with her son, injecting his veins with animosity, feeding him bottles full of a secret formula, referring to his father as foolish and obstinate, emphasizing that it was through her connections rather than his scientific talent or family position that he now lived, or could live, in a substantial house on the beautiful new boulevard. She did not allow Nehemiah to see his son, and he yearned for the two of them.

How he longed to touch, to see, to feel! How he yearned for

the cold and beautiful face of Shlomzion, secluded in her room, feeding a secret formula in sterile bottles; the gurgling sounds, the cooing and cuddling while dressing and undressing an infant whose form was unknown to him. He was tormented by the locked door, the scent of perfume, the stench of baby urine blending with the smell of sour milk, while inside the room sat Shlomzion the Great suffused with stormy passions, lulled by a tangle of enmity. Nehemiah sat on the boulevard which was still not quite a boulevard, his face craving, his eyes sparkling dolefully as he sang: They say there is love in the world; where is my love?

With the exception of Adonsky, no one was allowed to enter the house. Everyone, from the milkman to Little Mother Shlomzion, who was thrown out five times though her arms were laden with gifts for the baby, was regarded by Shlomzion as a potential spy. Nehemiah got thinner and thinner. He was heard mumbling esoteric words to himself on the boulevard lined with newly planted trees that were knee high. A number of benches had been set up along the avenue which was no longer a boulevard since the strollers were beginning to say: Let's call this Avenue Rothschild, like in Paris! Nehemiah sat on a freshly painted bench opposite his house, yearning for his wife whose window was locked from within.

After eight months of cold and quiet belligerence this saga became the town's principal subject of conversation. In the outlying settlements, as well as in distant Jerusalem, the battle between Nehemiah and Shlomzion over "that one" was discussed more and more frequently. For Adonsky was a public figure and Nehemiah was the son of Simha, of blessed memory. Aunt Shlomzion the Great was, furthermore, a scion of Ben-Amram's family, a family that had lived in Hebron and Jerusalem for six generations.

It might as well be admitted that Aunt Shlomzion was justified in one respect: objectivity did not prevail in this matter. With the exception of Jerusalem, where the factions were almost balanced, opinions in the outlying settlements favored Nehemiah over Shlomzion four to one. In Tel Aviv and Jaffa the score was approximately the same. Such was the typical street-corner exchange: What sort of name is that? Why this weird Biblical name anyway? Since when does a woman shut out her husband and torment him when he loves her dearly? She should accept his authority, they argued. Simha was a good man, by the standards of his time, so why not Simha? And on and on.

Shlomzion's virtues did not sustain her in the contest over public opinion. The campaign was waged on street corners, in the avenue, on the new benches, in the various parliaments that were beginning to form on the avenue or under the big tree which is now Mugrabi Square but was then a spot one would head for to walk, to be close to the sea, to relax on the distant seashore.

Adonsky hired fifty Arabs from Ramleh and a dozen Jews from Jerusalem—at the rate of two and a half grush a day plus two mill overtime for the Arabs and three and a half grush plus three mill overtime for the Jews—to post themselves on street corners, at the big tree and at the shore in order to establish the justice of Shlomzion's position at the major terminals of opinion. They argued: Wondrous-Counsel-Prince of Peace is a splendid name; if it was good enough for the son of Israel's greatest prophet, it should be good enough for Nehemiah. A woman is the mother of her child and man should subordinate his will to hers, all the more so in this case. Shlomzion's first child was defective because of her husband's contaminated blood and, in view of this, she wants her second child to be closely associated with prophetic vision. Repeatedly, they related the tale of Simha, the fool who bought a lot for a bishlik and, rather than bargain, sold it for the same price, proving which side of the family was the source of intelligence and which the source of madness. They described the anguish of the mother, of the poor baby, enclosed in his room, deprived of a father's compassion. One Jerusalemite expounded excitedly, all but singing his words: Woman—man! Womb-man . . . Considering her *woe*/man surely must *owe*/his wife/(the source of life)/respect and compassion. As any fool can see it is love-cum-passion that makes the womb-an whole.

The action was fierce, the arguments violent. Opinions

changed only slightly, despite the overtime, the polemics and disputations. The citizens of our town were not persuaded and the small number who wavered in their faith, tending first in one direction then in another, did not significantly alter the balance of opinion which was lining up solidly against Shlomzion and against her father, Adonsky.

When "that one" reached the age of eighteen months and began walking, chattering, sitting on the potty (Adonsky reported this proudly, at the tree), and when Shlomzion took him for a walk surrounded by her father's Arabs, to guard against Nehemiah and his cohorts, people pointed at him and said: Here comes Wondrous-Counsel, the nameless one! Or, There's Shlomzion with Prince-Peacey. But all this notwithstanding, the outcome of the struggle was predictable. An overwhelming majority contended that Aunt Shlomzion would prevail, perhaps in compromise form. Rumors of compromise began to circulate when the Jews from Jerusalem demanded a raise in salary and overtime. Adonsky, knowing that the Arabs would soon demand a raise, allowed these rumors to spread and wield their influence.

The battle over my cousin's name lasted eighteen months. Shlomzion and Nehemiah slept in separate rooms. She made a door directly to the outside so she could avoid the hall, locked the door to her own room and leaned an icebox against it to secure it. Nehemiah could not have gained entrance even if he had tried. But he was a proud man, and his tears were seen only by the sands of the avenue. Eighteen months of torment and weeping through countless cold nights and stifling heat as well: Shlomzion, Shlomzion! Choked by bitter loneliness, he began to worry about his sanity, his very life, to find it devoid of meaning. Losing hope, he suffered like a youth in unrequited love. He collected stamps in silence, dried and pasted enthusiastically, bathed in the sea in winter, danced wildly at a Hanukkah ball, rode north to Galilee on a rainy winter night, composed two long poems which he copied fifteen times in his flowing hand. One day he came to Mother Shlomzion, grabbed her picture of Grandfather Simha and tore it to shreds. Then he sat on the porch with Mother and talked for two whole days about the soft cheeks, full breasts, smooth hair of Shlomzion the Great. Mother poured him some cognac, a special bottle she was keeping for my wedding day, a gift received long ago from the head of the Rishon vineyards. In a drunken daze, Nehemiah made the rounds of the few but pleasant streets of the first Hebrew city in two thousand years, a white city, its houses like blocks of sweet chocolate, its back to the waves, strolling midst trees and flowers, shouting: Flowers for the head of a scoundrel! . . ."Is not my son so dear to me, Wondrous-Counsel-Prince of Peace!". . ."My brothers have dealt deceitfully! . . ." He ambled back and forth chanting: It's a long way to Tipperary; it's a sure way to die! And another song, invented that night: Glory, glory, hallelujah . . . Iceboxes on the rockses. Death to the iceboxes. Death to the rockses . . . Glory, glory, hallelujah! . . . How he yearned for his wife and child, for their touch, and scent, the fine man Nehemiah was.

After eighteen months, when the trees in the avenue were waist high and Adonsky's Arabs were demanding an increment for overtime which was met with total rejection, the letter was received. This letter, written by Nehemiah's wife, was sent via registered mail without a return address. It was notarized and hand-delivered to Nehemiah by the postmaster himself, and contained Shlomzion's proposal, which she said was a singularly generous proposal, the first and last. The proposed armistice, so said the letter, could serve as a prelude to peace and perhaps even to final conciliation, but should it be rebuffed, eternal belligerence would ensue and it would become impossible ever to come to terms.

She proposed that they call their son Arpahshad. Uncle Nehemiah was weary. Everyone was aware that he was right, even Adonsky's Arabs. He longed for Shlomzion and the child, and there were moments when it was as if he forgot, or was inclined to forget, the grounds for the war. He almost forgot his father's name, the very existence of the word *simha* (joy) in the Hebrew language; he began hating happy people because they reminded him of his father's name. On one such occasion he saw two boys carousing on Allenby Street and jumped them. One of Adonsky's Arabs broke up the fight. Nehemiah was becoming frail and depleted. He was willing to call his son Rudolph Valentino, Jehoahaz, Czar Nikolai, Marx, Spencer . . . anything.

At this point Adonsky informed his daughter that her supporters were dwindling whereas her enemies were gathering strength; that the wage demands reflected the insolence of a mindless mob acting against its own interests. Aunt Shlomzion read in the newspaper about preparations for the approaching Purim Ball. She realized that there had never been nor would there ever be a Queen Esther to equal her; that it was therefore essential that she reclaim the title of Queen, offering herself to Ahasuerus for the sake of her people. She regarded her son as her primary investment in the eternity of Israel. And, truly, why should she not be crowned before the eyes of her detractors? A compromise with respect to Wondrous-Counsel-Prince of Peace would surely facilitate matters. Her father agreed wholeheartedly.

Exhausted from the hostilities, Nehemiah was by now incapable of reading letters soberly. Neither did he follow the practice of his fellow citizens who spent the cold March nights that entire week repeating: Nehemiah is falling, Nehemiah is falling from down to doom. He didn't laugh with the others, nor did he respond with hilarity to the sound of such pet names as Arpahshady or Arpahshadinka. Bursting with suppressed passion, he ran to Shlomzion's room. The door was locked, secured by the weight of the icebox. The air was filled with the yearned-for fragrance of perfume, baby's urine, sour milk from a secret formula. He found a note bearing his name tacked on the door. He tore it off and read:

To Whom This May Concern—

The party agreeing to the name proposed in a letter dated March 15th of this year is required to present a notarized letter of apology stating that the name Arpahshad is acceptable (to him) and that the name Simha, which he proposed in a moment of weakness, was a perverse idea designed to batter the wife (of the aforesaid agreeable party, if he is agreeable!) who has endured severe hardship in her lifetime and brought an infant into this world for the sole purpose of providing the agreeing party with an heir to carry his name forward; that the name (Simha) was proposed deliberately and with the purpose of discrediting a solid citizen of the land, daughter of a family of rabbis and founding fathers, granddaughter of a noted Hebron scholar, with the intent to slander a woman before countless persons who regard Simha, father of the agreeing party, as a ludicrous figure, devoid of vision, who made improper advances to his female students, rode a crooked-legged donkey and sold Jewish land to Gentiles. The very thought of Shlomzion's son as bearer of this man's name is an aberration, indignity and an embarrassment to its perpetrator. The agreeing party must proclaim himself fully penitent and declare that he loves his wife with a blazing passion.

This letter should be written in triplicate: a copy for Adonsky; one copy for his legal wife (Shlomzion née Adonsky) (on pink paper to be found in the upper drawer of the guest-room bureau); and one to the beloved son who has been without a name in the eternal Land of Israel for eighteen months and who is totally unaquainted with his progenitor.

With declining respect,
Shlomzion

Nehemiah tried in vain to break down the door. He shouted but there was no response. He put on a jacket and tie and raced to Rehov Yehudah Ha-Levi, but the notary was already gone. He went to the notary's home in Jaffa, paid twice the ordinary fee, wrote three copies of the letter (one in pink), sniffed the garlic breath of the notary, who was in pajamas, eating with one hand while the other wrought the work, and sent the letter via registered mail.

After two days the barriers were broken. Uncle Nehemiah and Aunt Shlomzion were together again in their beautiful bedroom.

The war was over. The compromise was accepted all around and my cousin's name is now: Arty Brand.

Aunt Shlomzion the Great didn't give an inch. For twenty-eight years now she has been writing to him in America addressing him as Arpahshad Yacobi, though the letters are returned to her with the envelope stamped in English: ADDRESSEE UNKNOWN. She collected the letters that were returned, tied them with a pink ribbon and placed them on her chest of drawers. In the end, my cousin broke down, went to the post office and arranged to receive letters addressed to Arpahshad Yacobi. He reads them and flings them into the fire in winter, the trash in summer. Once, when I was drunk in Naples, in the company of a naked lady who sang bewitching Neopolitan songs while we ate cannoli on her bare belly with a view of Vesuvius out the window, I wrote my cousin a fine letter about the singing doll in my bed, about Naples, Vesuvius, Pompeii, the magnificent cannoli. I sent the letter to Arpahshad Yakobi. It was returned to me after a year, its envelope marked ADDRESSEE UNKNOWN, in my cousin's hand.

Arty Brand stammers even in his letters. He once sent me a letter begun one winter and concluded the next, a total of fifteen sentences explaining why he was marrying the woman his mother referred to as "the Shanghai whore." I sent him a picture of a nude with a snake entering the woman's marvelous places, a picture he had once bought in Jaffa and left with me.

Aunt Shlomzion says her son will bring her to an untimely end. The traitor, she says, looking longingly at pictures of Uncle Nehemiah and Adonsky; he lives in America with a whore from Shanghai and is killing his mother, step by step.

Why Shanghai? I ask.

Because the fool escaped from Russia to Japan. And from there to America.

But why Shanghai, Aunt Shlomzion?

What was there for her to do in Japan? Is that a place for Jews? Aunt Shlomzion asked, continuing to hate the world with chilly yearning.

7

On the bureau in the private hospital in north Tel Aviv Aunt Shlomzion's two beloveds stand framed in gold. The expression in the eyes of the gray-haired doctor reminds me of all of Shlomzion's acquaintances: yearning, adulation and eagerness for the day of reckoning. Nehemiah and Adonsky, framed in gold, seem so pleasant next to her, so remote from hostility, complementing rather than rivaling each other. Uncle Nehemiah is in official dress in this photograph, from 1952, when he served as roving ambassador to Europe. He looks absurd, like some scrawny kid masquerading as an English nobleman—poor Sir Moses Montefiore—or a peddler, perhaps. Wearing a top hat, holding a parchment copy of Israel's Declaration of Independence, he recedes into a bold montage of the Western Wall, the Tomb of Rachel Our Mother, Ben-Gurion, Herzl on the bridge at the first Zionist Congress, two children planting trees, a coin from Bar Kochba's time, the insignia of Israel's Defense Forces, kibbutz Nir-David in the early days of furtive colonization. Herzl's pale and misty image merges with the lines of Rachel's tomb, with

Ben-Gurion's searing gaze and a view of the dim greenish horizon of Nir-David in the early morning.

The second photograph: Adonsky himself. He, too, is formally dressed, but the style suits him well; his attire seems fitting and appropriate; he holds a gold-tipped scepter. His image is set against a montage of houses in Beirut, the Mosque of Omar, the Church of the Holy Sepulcher, the Empire State Building, a brandy seal indicating excellence from an international competition in Liechtenstein in 1899, two stone lions, a woman in black, a tin of oil, a dim arm embracing the woman as well as the tin, two splendid peacocks with an emblem flowing from their silvered beaks: Yusuf Mahmud—certified artistic photographer.

The two profiles face each other as though Adonsky and Nehemiah were engaging in conversation across ancient battlements, from positions of uncontestable strength, like two paper field marshals backed up by vast empires.

In the faded photo Uncle Nehemiah's eyes look bright yet suffused with a dusky film of sweetness. In life my uncle had dark brown eyes, almost black, set in violet pits, like Aunt Shlomzion's eyes.

They had identical lines on the palms of their right hands. Fortune-tellers marveled at this. They both had a long life line and lines of character and affect that matched. Nehemiah and Aunt Shlomzion the Great had dimples in the same spot on the left cheek; their height was identical, as was the bright olive cast of their skin as well as their hair color. In fact, they both began turning gray on the same day. It was Arbor Day, 1948, Shlomzion recalled: We were in the yard. We looked at each other and exclaimed, A white hair! It was a fine day, the beginning of spring. The almond tree in Mr. Kvisky's yard had just burst into bloom, like in the books.

The photograph is so unflattering that my uncle looks like a pauper who has somehow acquired an aristocratic father. The photograph of Adonsky, on the other hand, was a true likeness: king of himself in vain, not unlike the writer of these pages. This, perhaps, explains my weakness for his daughter and for him.

Adonsky, says Aunt Shlomit, in one of those moments of recurring sadness that follow every frustrating attempt to call on Shlomzion the Great, would like to be a henchman in the court of Ibrahim Pasha or in the secret recesses of the Taj Mahal. But that's a building in India, Aunt Shlomit, I observe. Then in the Empire of Abdullah or of King Ahab! I smile: Shlomit, Shlomit. Ahab was certainly Adonsky's king. You guessed it this time. My aunt sits on the terrace tending plants. Fermentation . . . But why all the hate? She thinks but doesn't understand; she tries—oh, how she tries—year after year! Still drawn to Shlomzion though she is repeatedly rejected. Ahab, Adonsky's king. Shlomzion the Great, like Jezebel: daughter and mistress, daughter of Sidon and mother, sprung from Adonsky's loins. How many of Jaffa's women swear that they saw Shlomzion being born of her father, not her mother? Ahab, Adonsky would have told Asael, an intimate of Mother's, was a giant who decided to forgo his position in history as builder of empires, commander of mighty armies with tens of thousands of chariots, spectacular leader and renowned expert in non-liquid assets. Clowns like Simha, he said . . . clowns who sit in dungeons like Jeremiah and Simha, deliver speeches filled with reproach, get themselves stoned, wear sackcloth and sound off in broken rhyme, smash vessels and demoralize the people so that they leave their land. . . . Simha and his sort rewrite history, dedicating entire books to clowns and good-for-nothings they call prophets, being in awe of them and dazzled, while devoting a single chapter to the greatest of the kings. All because of a vineyard. What vineyard, why vineyard, Adonsky protested. What a perversion! And why not take the vineyard? he argued.

What did Naboth do with it anyway?

Every king has a coterie of flatterers and enemies. Petty zealots incensed by some Jezebel. Our entire educational system is distorted, he proclaimed. Joshua and Ahab should be emphasized, not Simha. There is no Book of Simha!

It would be a sad book. And Jeremiah! No? Adonsky became agitated but reverted instantly to his proverbial indifference. Golden francs began dancing in his eyes.

Shlomit doesn't understand. Why would she understand? We live in our own small sanctified world, she and I, inhabited by cardboard kings—Shlomzion, Ben-Amram, Adonsky—created for us. These words, Shlomit, were costly. Adonsky gave a hundred francs to the synagogue building fund. Only then was the threat of excommunication reversed. He muttered: Poets! Imagine buying a lot for a bishlik, then selling it. One can speak either of Naboth's vineyard or of David's conduct with Bathsheba. . . . Hypocrites.

Great people make history, he said; they have grand passions. Small people write about people who have grand passions and emasculate generations of children with their own impotence!

But these things were never said aloud. There was no further threat of excommunication. And Adonsky saved a hundred francs.

Adonsky always knew which side his bread was buttered on. He had dispatched word of his contribution to the new synagogue throughout Jaffa and gave public thanks to Messrs. Halfon, Kahanah, Liebman, Chitingov and Wallenrod for apprising him of his error and bringing him—through their great wisdom and generosity—to acknowledge it. Then he went to drink arak with the mayor of Jaffa and increased his synagogue contribution to two hundred francs. After this he proceeded to sell Assam Assani a lot at an exorbitant price. Assani, in turn, sold it to Messrs. Halfon, Kahanah, Liebman, Chitingov and Wallenrod at an even more inflated price. . . . Adonsky earned back his contribution with an additional 200 percent interest. Nor was Assam Assani any the worse for the deal.

So everyone was happy.

The mayor of Jaffa received a new narghile from Adonsky. The permit for construction of the synagogue was issued, complete with gold illumination and the signatures of five officials.

Shlomit calls this synagogue Naboth's Vineyard.

It was actually known as Simha's Vineyard, after Simha, son of Yehosef Tabib, author of *Abraham's Vineyard*, a work that challenged the opinions and tales of Shlomzion's grandfather, Rabbi Ben-Amram of Hebron, who disappeared with a sizable fund, taking with him secrets pertaining to the ten lost tribes and the mysterious Sambatyon River.

Naboth's Vineyard is a handsome enough structure, complete with white enamel spitoons. When Adonsky was honored by being called up, repeatedly, to read the Torah, so that people began grumbling and saying why doesn't he stay up there already, Aunt Shlomzion the Great decided that Naboth's Vineyard was in the lead.

Later, when the cholera epidemic began in Egypt, Adonsky walked five cigarettes' distance with his Arab, bought a plot of land, fenced it in and named it (to himself) the cholera plot. When the epidemic reached Jaffa as he had anticipated, having been brought in by laborers who came from Egypt to seek work in Palestine, and the Jews were afraid to bury their dead in Jaffa, his land was ready and waiting . . . in the dunes, far from everything. This spot is now known as the Old Cemetery of Tel Aviv. Only the most eminent and distinguished citizens are buried there.

Tel Aviv was built around it, spreading north and east. The plots are all taken; its population includes Adonsky himself, my Grandfather Simha, my two grandmothers. It was one of Adonsky's most spectacular acquisitions. Anyone who can predict the course of an epidemic deserves to make a lot of money, says Aunt Shlomzion the Great. Nevertheless, she adds, they teach about Henkin and Ruppin. Who mentions Adonsky? There are scoundrels in Tel Aviv who bought land for Zionist reasons, opposed Naboth's Vineyard, functioned on purely idealistic grounds, Shlomzion argues. And today, when a grandchild comes of age, these people sell one lot; when there is a wedding, they sell two. They own citrus groves and vineyards, are all highly respected, appear in every textbook dressed as pioneers, knapsacks slung over their backs, holding walking sticks for the pilgrimage to Palestine. Their words have become slogans. Songs commemorate them. Their pioneering qualities are celebrated in street names like Allenby, Montefiore, Dizengoff . . . Fathers of our country! And Adonsky, who bought more than anyone, buying for money rather than for Zionism, had to bring five hundred

Arabs to his own funeral. And they, who own hundreds of *dunams*, attract government heads, prominent ministers to their funerals, without pay. Even members of the diplomatic corps come, Aunt Shlomzion says. Is there justice in the world? Naboth's Vineyard?

If there was justice in the world, says Aunt Shomit, Shlomzion would dismember it. What is justice to her? In a just world she would lose her bearings and disintegrate like a wilted flower. She is an agitating force, seething with vitality. She could serve as a glorious test tube, a source for penicillin. With her beautiful eyes she would restore the healthy. And so Aunt Shlomit drinks black coffee in a melancholy mood. She is on the brink of despair, in love with her old clock, waiting for the ring of the Redeemer.

8

Paris, 1952. Aminadav is in Paris studying. He lives on tomato peel in a room in Cité Flager. The cold-water faucets are in the courtyard near Suzanne's room, Suzanne with the wild hair. No blankets in winter; a vicious old concierge who reeks of garlic and scolds: If you're cold, I'm always here. Her eyes are bright and dead. Nehemiah was roving ambassador to Europe at the time, and Aminadav was hungry. A year of shaving with cold water in the yard does not exactly make one's skin tender. The nights are cold; work is difficult. Paris is hostile and haunted by memories of war. The Americans with their G.I. Bill lead a wild life.

When Nehemiah and Shlomzion arrived in Paris for their official visit, Aminadav received an invitation to meet with the Ambassador in front of the Opéra at noon on Tuesday. Everyone helped to prepare him for the event, outfitting him handsomely, instructing him in the graces of eating in chic restaurants, the order of courses, how many salads to eat to develop an appetite, how much wine to drink, how to dip your hands in warm water at the end of the meal. Everyone was excited on his behalf. It was hardly an everyday occurrence for someone from Cité Flager to dine at Maxim's or at Tour d'Argent, to meet with diplomats, ride in a Rolls-Royce.

At the Opéra Aminadav kissed Shlomzion's broad powdered cheek and clutched Nehemiah's hand warmly. They were both dressed in solid well-tailored English clothes. Nehemiah wore a black hat. They seemed unrelated to the boulevard where the beautiful people ambled toward cafés, toward American Express. Nehemiah asked how things were going. Aminadav said so-so. ... Things are going well enough, but— She cut in to say: Ami looks awful. It was a bleak autumn day and Aunt Shlomzion, whose great moment occurred that autumn day when the French ship fired five shells at the factory of Wagner, the German, loved autumn days. Her mood was good. She said: Ami looks awful, rather than Ami looks like a rag, or: Why doesn't that stingy mother of his send him some money?

Cars glisten in the pale sunlight. Flocks of pigeons drift past framed by walls painted in bold colors. Exquisite women fill the cafés. Gentlemen in suits and gloves wink at these beautiful creatures made of crystal. Aminadav is in a state of anticipation. He looks all around. The scene is like an old picture postcard of Paris. Nehemiah says: So? It's not easy? She interrupts again, and Nehemiah seeks the meaning of his life in the cracks of the sidewalk. She says: You could help us, Ami. Nehemiah is tired of these revolting tourist restaurants, with flaming crêpe suzettes, waiters who look like clowns and reek of eau de Cologne. We're tired of eating snails, frogs' legs, spiders in disgusting sauces. Nehemiah wants you to take him to a simple students' restaurant. You know, Ami, a folksy place, the Parisian version of Tnuva, back home. We want to remember who we are. We're fed up with all this pretense.

Nehemiah refuses to look up. Ami can't possibly catch his eye. Let's go, she said.

Aminadav was baffled for a moment, swallowed his expectations and said yes.

Uncle Nehemiah looked as though he had been fished out of the water, depressed and worn. His hat seemed pasted on; his face had the marks of rare fatigue. Webs of shame? He didn't know. Aminadav pitied Nehemiah, who was dressed like an aging prince. So smooth, agreeable and handsome against the backdrop of the striking Opéra building. I could take him to my room and show him how I live, he thought; who I am, the conditions of my life. He would be shocked. But Shlomzion would go home and tell Little Mother Shlomzion (and anyone else who might be interested) that Aminadav lives off the profit of whores, in a cheap brothel, a filthy den of iniquity, concluding in a shattered tone: See what you get when you desert your homeland?

Let's take a taxi, Aminadav said, with innocence characteristic of Little Shlomzion's son. I know a good cheap student restaurant.

But just then Aunt Shlomzion remembered a trip she took with Nehemiah twenty-five years back, how they had lived in Paris, loved riding the Métro. Third class, she added—with those charming Parisians.

They have changed since then, Aminadav offered. But she didn't hear, or pretended not to hear. I want to see them, she said. We want to be people again. We're tired of all the stuffed shirts —right, Nehemiah?

He mumbled something into the sidewalk, laden with history. They went down to the Métro.

Third class was jammed, without an inch to spare. Nehemiah suffered in silence. Shlomzion suffered out loud. How can they bear this: stinking of garlic and onion, living in crowds, bathing twice a month—like Jews from our slums, from Shuq Ha-Carmel. Nehemiah was alarmed and began reading his English newspaper avidly. She screamed: Nehemiah, you're ruining your eyes! How many times have I told you not to read when in motion! Remember at Lord Bevensruk's? How many times did I yell at you then? But you insist on behaving like a child. She turned to Aminadav: I can't trust him. I have to watch him all the time. He forgets he's not just anybody. He represents Israel in the world, like Herzl. He's killing himself. Nehemiah folded the newspaper and groaned into his hand, a silent groan that filled Aminadav with longing for his home, his youth. Only he could have heard it. A groan that was familiar from distant days, when Nehemiah used to show Aminadav his stamps and Shlomzion would suddenly barge in and say: It's time to go home. Your mother is waiting. And besides, Nehemiah is busy and too polite to tell you so. My own poor dear!

He absorbed the communication and all but smiled into the car filled with humanity and its foul stench.

The restaurant was crowded with painters, young and old. There was a line waiting for tables. The proprietor, who knew Aminadav, was wiping a table with a filthy cloth. They sat down and were approached by a waiter whose white coat was stained, his hair greasy. They were served thin soup, overcooked vegetables, *vin ordinaire*, an unconvincing cheese. Aunt Shlomzion would not allow them to order meat in such an unsanitary place. It must be full of microbes, she said, and, as you know, syphilis is common here in France. It's worth being checked by a doctor. It's a serious disease. You should guard your health, at least as long as your mother is alive. Nehemiah has a delicate stomach, she added, while waiting for him to pay. She examined each coin before letting him hand it to the waiter, and salvaged two francs he was about to add to the tip.

He doesn't know which end is up, she explained to Aminadav on the way out, stuffing the francs into her purse. It's awful how the French eat, she said, sounding worried about the future of the French people. Aminadav tried to smile at Nehemiah, whose adeptness at evading his glance was positively breathtaking.

They went to a café. There was a faded sign in the corner: JEWS AND DOGS FORBIDDEN. The proprietor has a weakness for history, Shlomzion remarked. Later, when she went to the bathroom (explaining in English: I'm going to powder my nose!), Nehemiah leaned over and spoke quickly, his eyes brimming with affection. He said: I know; it must be awful. Tell me how things are. No money?

Aminadav spoke quickly, too: The situation is bad. Nothing to eat. The grant hasn't come through yet. But it will come. Meanwhile, can you lend me some money? I can't pay the rent. I haven't eaten a real meal in a month. And I don't have anyone to turn to.

Nehemiah took out his wallet hurriedly and was rummaging through the pile of sterling when Shlomzion appeared. The powdering had been accomplished speedily. Nehemiah paled and pretended to be toying with the wallet, absent-mindedly. She proclaimed in a loud voice: Nehemiah, that's government money!

It's mine, he retorted, straining his words.

It's the government's!

It's mine.

I'm tired of looking after you, Nehemiah. You're not a baby. You represent a poor country and Little Shlomzion, who is known for her connections with the black market, could send a little money to her adorable son. He's sick with syphilis, and before you know it he'll lose all his limbs. Considering her involvement with the underworld, Little Shlomzion could easily arrange to transfer Israeli funds and exchange them on the black market. That's not your job. You have official duties.

He was bewildered. Aminadav felt sorry for him. As well as for her.

She continued: There's no need to hide anything from Ami. He knows his mother as well as you and I do. Besides, if he wanted to earn money like a straight and decent person, he would have stayed home and found work. But he wanted to go to Paris, to abandon his country in these difficult times. You know about artists, of course. He, after all, wants to be an artist, which is appropriate for Simha's grandson. An artist must experience hunger— He insists on being an artist, but I doubt that he will succeed because in the end it takes some talent, too, not just starvation! Everyone knows that a hungry artist with two ears isn't equipped to draw, with or without talent. In fact, Rembrandt cut off his ears and ate them. And didn't Tolstoy devour the apples he drew?

Nehemiah said: The grant hasn't come yet, and he doesn't have anything to eat.

That's good! Period. It suits his temperament. Simha's rightful heir. All these young people deserting their country—who will be left?

Nehemiah tried to get a word in.

Aminadav didn't even try.

Why did we establish a state? she said.

Nehemiah tried a new tactic: Aminadav fought for his country's independence and was wounded. . . . Didn't he earn it? Didn't he earn the chance to study?

Painting? A new state needs painters? Let him study agriculture, construction, chemistry. Why painting? Let him work the land. Adonsky bought land and reclaimed deserts. Who will live there? Jews are studying in Paris and Arabs live on lands acquired by Adonsky. Why is he suddenly so deserving? What does Adonsky deserve for fifty years of service to his people? Was a street named for him? These scoundrels forget quickly. His mother is to blame. She knows Ben-Gurion, Remez and Finstuck from the Revenue Department. She advises them: Don't name a street for Adonsky! She's fighting Simha's battle and sending her son to Paris—to draw whores, to pass the hat, to beg for charity. The new Jew! Emancipated. Tolstoy from Ben Yehuda Street, wandering through our dunes. . . .

Shlomzion drags Nehemiah outside. A breeze is blowing. Cars speed by. The houses look gray. Thin rain begins to fall.

Nehemiah stops for a minute to button his coat, slips his hand into his pocket, takes out a pack of Player's cigarettes, stuffs a bill into it (using his coat to mask this move), drops the box and motions Aminadav to pick it up. Shlomzion is busy with her hat. Aminadav represses his expression of gratitude.

Nehemiah whispered: Don't worry, I'll send you more. This is for now. Every night she counts the money in my wallet. I'll tell her I lost the bill.

I hope she believes you, Aminadav said.

He kissed Aunt Shlomzion on the cheek. She said: Give my

regards to your mother and buy yourself a new coat. You look very bad. We'll send you a postcard—right, Nehemiah? And don't forget to visit your old aunt. Before leaving she added: I have to sleep this afternoon. We're having dinner with the French Foreign Minister. The Louvre? There's nothing worth looking at there . . . Egyptian sculpture and drawings by anti-Semites. I need my sleep, Nehemiah. You can work on tomorrow's lecture.

Shlomzion is a beautiful woman, Aminadav thinks. Beautiful as the sharp eye of an eagle.

9

I met old Nahumi, the teacher, on Wednesday. He was walking the streets, tired, a man whose footsteps were lost, seeking Shlomzion in vain. Nahumi, who remembers Little Mother Shlomzion from her days in the drama club, many years back, when she played the role of Shulamit, asks after my aunt. He is afraid to visit the hospital. Why see all that suffering? I can't do it, he says. It's so unnecessary.... I think about my own gnarled body. How much longer will I be here? I'm afraid. You laugh at me?

No, I said. I, too, am afraid.

I described the hospital room, Shlomzion's huge empty house, the key under her pillow. We spoke of Nehemiah's uniforms, the feud over my cousin's name, the gold-plated birdcages that never housed a bird, the beautiful paintings hanging there with no one to look at them. I said, all of a sudden, with a trace of wickedness suited to others that just then enticed me as well: She lies there contemplating the cost of her room, depleting the anticipated inheritance at the rate of sixteen lirot an hour. Imagine Amihud M. turning gray.

Nahumi does not respond in this vein. He seems burdened by remote visions, by the non-rational, occupied with distant birds on streets that no longer exist, baffled by years with which I never was acquainted, as if time were the only thing of substance in the world. He says: One must understand Shlomzion; she has an element of glory. She remains a broken idol, in ruins, aging like an ancient palace! I quote Emerson: Man is God in ruins.

Nahumi took out a notebook, leafed through it excitedly, his hands trembling. He arrived at a page labeled SHLOMZION (C) and jotted down my words. He asked me to write the phrase for him in English. I obliged. Magnificent, he said, putting the notebook back in his pocket. So right: it expresses Shlomzion to perfection, in all her glory, glory from the Lord of the world; a word invested with passion and storm.

We drank juice and were silent. Afterward I reflected that all of us, all those who knew her (with the exception of her son Arty Brand), find something to love in her, something we cannot identify. We are all captivated by the charm of her wild temperament, its singularity. Her wickedness enthralls us.

Nahumi said: Did you know she entrusted old Abrams with the key to her involuted finances?

The judge in the hospital in Raanana?

Yes.

Do you know why?

I didn't know.

The man is old, very old, and he has seen that his dream is ending, too. What is he now? A broken implement. My age. Half his body is paralyzed. They have to sit him on the pot. Poor fellow. He hasn't a living soul. Alone and solitary. Long ago, in this city, didn't we all have a dream? You heard the speeches at the funeral? We were dreamers. Everyone searching for a corner. We were links in a chain. There was something astonishing in the air. How did you put it? God in ruins? There are traces of God's ruins in all of us. I speak somewhat like a teacher—I was, in fact, a teacher for fifty-two years. So much youth withered in my hands. If my language is inflated, forgive me. I see the world as it is today—television, raucous boys, long hair. I find it impossible to understand . . . the verbal harshness, the violence of words. No tenderness, no mystery. No wonder or genuine amazement. Everything exposed and promiscuous. The girls I taught to dance blossomed in my hands. These blooms were picked by young men who grew mustaches and sang patriotic songs: "God will build the Galilee," and "in blood and fire Judea fell,/in blood and fire Judea will arise. . . ." Times change . . . years pass. Where was I? Abrams doesn't even know the clue is in his hands? And if he knew, would he know why?

Nahumi had some more juice. The day was pleasant. Flowers fell from the crowns of the purple trees. He reflected: The land that looked chaste when it was being rebuilt has assumed the face of an overly made-up gypsy. Tall buildings. Cars. Noise. Misunderstanding. Indifference. Spacious houses. Roads. Government. But the dream can't be taken away! I'm an old man, guarding the dream. My brother, you know, abandoned this land in the twenties. He went off to America where he sold shirts. He said to me, Why suddenly this urge to build and be rebuilt on a land infested with mites and Arabs? He sneered at me, Aminadav. He built castles out of shirts in a place called Long Island. Shlomzion said it's a nice place. I never left this country. The day I arrived here, I was fourteen at the time, I vowed I would never leave. And, in fact, I never did leave. Not for a single day. I live in a small apartment on Rehov Maletz. Such noise, Aminadav. One day there was a meeting. I saw it announced in a magazine. Everyone was there, at the Mann Auditorium. Have you seen that magnificent structure? They looked prosperous, well dressed, arriving in grand cars. Golda was there. I, of course, remember when she arrived in Jaffa. We were at the harbor watching Jews get off the boat. Those were depressed days, a period when many left and few came. Everyone came to the meeting, a charming event, endless speeches about the good old days. Golda said the best days of her life were spent in the small kitchen in Merhavia. Sapir spoke too. He was young when we took his closest friend to the Galilee. We were on horseback then, Aminadav. It was a dream in which Sapir was still Koslovsky. Golda recalled the malaria and the mosquitoes. My eyes filled with tears. We were one family then. Not Adonsky, not Shlomzion, but all the rest of us. Your mother! Your grandfather. There were great personalities. Everyone stared at me. I looked out of place. I suddenly realized that I didn't belong. My back was bent; I had no chauffeured limousine. I was dressed like my grandfather.

Nahumi raised his voice and bellowed: I went to see Golda when the meeting was over. She was surrounded. I turned to her: Hello, Golda. She said a broad hello, but her eyes did not light up! She didn't recognize me. Her bodyguards pushed me away. I wanted to remind her of the time she slipped in the mud and I . . . But they shoved me aside and searched my pockets. They took me away, Aminadav, and checked me thoroughly. A security check for old Nahumi, who taught the Shertok sisters folk dancing even before World War I. Am I some Arab terrorist?

Golda smiled at all sorts of people, shards of people, not gods, and left. She didn't remember. But listen to this: when my brother came for a visit and decided to build himself a villa in Savyon . . . Did I tell you about that? No? He made himself a housewarming party, my beloved brother—from his shirt empire. He sent a chauffeured car to pick me up. I didn't want it, but he insisted. I arrived at a palace, Aminadav. Everything was marble, gleaming, complete with Chinese servants from Hong Kong. They looked Japanese, bowing, spouting: *Tenk yu, tenk yu.* Everything was *tenk yu.* I asked for fruit juice! They said: *Tenk yu.* She was there—Golda. And Sapir was there, too. As well as all the generals. And writers. Darting around my cherished brother. They came to feast on his disgust. It wasn't only shirts that built his empire, you know. Fifty years devoted to the oppression of widows and orphans, building homes for the aged and stealing their food. On Long Island. Now he was here to watch all these Zionists grovel before the golden shirt idol. So respectful! He smiles at me and says in Russian: See them dancing around me! The head of your government herself is in a whirl! And you, he says, have been here sixty years, dried swamps, eaten anopheles, were building and being built à la Pinsker, Berl and all your other social philosophers. What's the matter with you?

Do you need someone to put in a good word with Sapir, to arrange a better apartment for you? I am a prominent Zionist. I have a roomy pocket and you, after all, are my dear brother! My own brother was mocking me. . . .

He was right. I went home to Maletz Street, sat at the window, watched some children beating a cat. Still, Aminadav, Nahumi shrieked, they can't deprive me of the dream! They can't wrench that away from me! What we wanted was beautiful, unique. Someone once said that an idea can't be responsible for those who adopt it. . . . So Golda and Sapir are there and I am still here! Each one of us had a great moment around which we constructed an entire life. Some holy community from Russia or Poland enclosed by high walls—is that Zionism? A Defense Ministry with a Philharmonic Orchestra? Are these the great responses of the Jewish people? It takes generations to be redeemed! Not just for me, for Golda as well. But it was worth it. For that single moment. It was worthwhile even for your Aunt Shlomzion!

He was silent, lost in thought. His face was very handsome now, radiant, soft. Which moment? I asked.

He studied me at some length. Birds fluttered through the clear air. The purple flowers were still falling. Life is beautiful or ugly, long or short, he said, but there is neither justice nor injustice beyond what we do with ourselves, whether we fulfill some destiny or, perhaps, if we are lucky, become our own selves. Aunt Shlomzion is full of hate, never repents, is sly as a serpent. There was that moment that formed her, carved her in space. A moment she craves. Note the economy of our language. Carve and crave. Serpent, repent . . . Her life carved; her moment craved. I already told you about Abrams, the elderly judge in the hospital in Raanana. He's nearly ninety. He once rode a donkey from Petah Tikva to Jaffa; to pick flowers. Abrams used to dry flowers. In those days he was known as Vladya Abramsky. He saw Shlomzion—she was sixteen at the time—a few seconds after the French ship fired five shells in the direction of Wagner's factory. It was the ultimate moment of Shlomzion's life. She described it to me later, saying: Nahumi, you are an amusing man, a funny fellow with irrelevant dreams, like spiders' webs that froze. I had one sublime moment, Nahumi, and years later I revealed my secret to the one person who saw me then, when I was happy for the first and last time in my life. . . . And he, Abrams, has no idea why she entrusted him with it. But I know, Nahumi says, dreaming Shlomzion with tearful eyes. He concludes: She's a hard woman, Aminadav. . . . Still, have you ever seen anyone more beautiful?

No, I admitted.

There is a gentle link between evil and wealth. I am certain of this. She has everything: money, honor, cruelty, power, wit, guile. Are you an heir, Aminadav?

No.

And does Little Mother Shlomzion appear in the will?

Who knows? But I imagine not. Mother is certain the answer is no.

And how about me? He smiled, a broken sheepish smile.

You? I laughed. Why you?

She may have no further wish to crush me. Why? Won't she leave anything for me to dream? Even a dream of my dream? Sleepless nights? No. I'll die before her. We'll all die before her. Her will must contain fragments of that singular moment in Jaffa when she was sixteen, along with receipts for five million dollars.

Will there be anything left? I suddenly began to worry.

She'll leave her money to the Land of Israel, Nahumi speculated in a tone that was so distracted that it seemed to come from another era to inhabit Nahumi's dream, the dream that expired at the party for the cherished brother with the orphanages, and with Golda dancing round the golden calf.

Old Nahumi got up and began walking, his back bent, seeking his own footsteps on the sidewalk. He returned, like the Nelly Sachs hero, without footsteps. He didn't even take leave of me. He went to Shlomzion's house, stood at the locked gate, across from the large garden full of weeds and tired vines laden with untrimmed tendrils, his eyes all tenderness and yearning.

10

And now for an account of that most singular moment in the life of Aunt Shlomzion the Great, as related by Nahumi to Little Mother Shlomzion and by Little Mother Shlomzion to me. I, in turn, relayed it to Arty Brand, her son. He laughed in disbelief, thinking I invented the story myself.

At the outbreak of the Great World War, Shlomzion was sixteen years old. One day she drove in Adonsky's magnificent carriage from Jaffa to Jamossin for a final visit to poor Hawaja Assam Kassani.

Assam Kassani had sold considerable acreage, many deeds and building permits to Adonsky, including various categories of land which—in theory, at least—were the property of the Ottoman government. Through devious channels fraught with adventure, Assam Kassani was able to obtain elaborately ornamented certificates, written in a fine curliced hand, from weary effendis who were passing their final days in Beirut, drinking arak with French virgins nestled on their quivering knees. Assam, a skilled and seasoned mediator, was consumed with anxiety. There was danger on every side: Jews, Turks, Arabs. He tried to be on good terms with all of them, but wasn't sure who would ultimately prevail. When young Arabs with whom he was casually acquainted began speaking of Greater Syria, referring to Palestine as southern Syria and writing vituperative articles against Jews, he went furtively to Zionist meetings to hear what ardent Zionists were saying about the Land of Zion, Anatoth and Shiloh. In the early days of Tel Aviv, when Adonsky remained in Jaffa refusing to take up residence in the small new settlement, Assam Kassani acquired a great deal of land on his behalf adjacent to the enormous field on which the first neighborhoods of Tel Aviv were constructed. Adonsky himself was aware of only two emotions. First was joy or sadness in response to the success or failure of a land enterprise; second was love for his daughter Shlomzion. Kassani, who knew him well, was generous with praise for Shlomzion. And, in fact, he did respect her and acknowledge her power. He was one of a few individuals who knew the identity of Jacobus Khon, in whose name the plot was acquired on which Tel Aviv was later founded. However, when the Turkish commander decided to build an army camp between Jaffa and the newly established settlement in order to abort the enterprise and undermine the new neighborhoods, and when the Muslim and Christian populations of Jaffa danced through the streets singing "down with the Jewish colony," Assam Kassani was among those who danced excitedly to the accompaniment of a wild chorus of flutes. In the heat of his gyrations he noticed Shlomzion's face in the window.

She was watching him. Her expression was cold and gloomy. Duly ashamed, he tried to appear drunk. She knew he wasn't drunk, and he knew she knew. She said to Adonsky, who was also observing the scene: I feel like Michal, daughter of Saul, watching King David prance like some clumsy youth, scorning him with nearly total satisfaction. Adonsky said: He made all that land available to me, Shlomzion. She smiled at her father like a mechanical doll, and Kassani, seeing her smile, waved to her and continued to celebrate the destruction of Tel Aviv with his brothers.

Adonsky said: Their joy is premature. They're unrealistic. This land rejects masters, will continue to cast them out as it has done from time immemorial, tolerating neither Jews nor Ishmaelites. Come, let's have some good coffee. Assam will dance; then he'll bring more certificates. He'll pay for his foolish performance. He knows that even the short-term victor has not been determined yet. In the long run a cruel god prevails, enemy of people and masters, lord of the bitter earth, king of non-liquid assets.

Assam Kassani lived in constant fear. When he was near death, Adonsky sent Herr Wolff, his German doctor, to look in on him. Herr Wolff was also Adonsky's only friend. Many years back, in his youth, he had crossed the desert on camelback, a year and a half's journey. Before that he had traveled through many lands as captain of a ship that plied the Pacific, had collected rare butterflies, which he pasted under glass, and had all but forgotten Cologne, his birthplace. As long as he was able to drink beer or good wine, he refused to bemoan his wasted years. He had a total of twenty-five children by eleven wives, leaving behind six male children, and daughters in several of our convents. His nightmare (on the rare occasions when he was sober) was that his sons and daughters, who were unknown to him, would appear at his fine house in Jaffa, which was surrounded by a huge garden, and knock on the door shouting, Father! He used to check the windows, bolt the doors and sit by the fire with a loaded gun in his hand, waiting in terror. An Arab boy once knocked on the door for help; the doctor fired at him. The boy later became his personal servant and tended his beautiful garden. His house was adjacent to the Jaffa church. On Sundays, Herr Wolff used to pray devoutly. In the afternoon he would write letters, in code, to a small mysterious office in Berlin. These letters, based on fact, were sophisticated and astute. No one understood the Jews of Israel, the Arabs of Palestine, the country's rulers, as well as he. Though he was most often seen in an inebriated state, his mind was brutal and slick, his vision acute, transcending the cloud of drunkenness. His pile of gold coins mounted month by month.

Herr Wolff, whose first name was unknown, had acquired medical knowledge while serving as the captain of a merchant ship on the Pacific. He enjoyed reading medical texts, and this made it possible for him to pose as a licensed doctor and even to succeed in situations where bona-fide practitioners had failed.

On that day when Shlomzion was formed by a singular moment of infinite bliss, Herr Wolff was riding to Assam Kassani for the purpose of a thoroughgoing (and final) checkup. Adonsky had paid him generously and issued precise instructions. There was no need for Kassani to engage in questions; the answers were inscribed on the doctor's forehead even before being asked. The doctor forced a smile, kissed Assam's blazing forehead, gave him medication and turned to ride homeward. It was morning. The day was enchanted and filled with fragrance. As he rode, he sang a song to himself, a Hebrew song he had learned from the young ladies of the school for girls whom he coveted so, though they avoided him. He sang: How lovely are the nights in Canaan—saying canon instead of Canaan.

At that very moment young Vladya Abramsky was picking flowers in Jaffa's citrus groves. He spied Herr Wolff in the distance, riding and singing in his German accent: How lovely are the nights in canon . . . He waved and continued gathering flowers, an array of wild blossoms, hidden beauties that seemed surprised in the moist earth, blooming early after a long summer and a short but rainy autumn.

And so it happened that while Vladya Abramsky was collecting flowers, passionately, and Herr Wolff was riding home singing a sentimental Hebrew song, Assam Kassani lay on his sickbed, vexed and bewildered, awaiting the approaching end.

He lay there, very pale in his white pajamas, something turbanlike on his head, mumbling prayers, fingering his amber beads, feverish and sad as he contemplated a meaningless eternity filled with the rustle of angels.

Herr Wolff returned to Adonsky, and Adonsky rushed off quickly to take leave of his dear dying friend, carrying with him a large sheet of paper that resembled parchment, in order to conclude the deal of his lifetime. He had been awaiting this moment for years, planning it carefully. When two foxes, veteran warriors, seasoned fighters, are aligned in the interest of the deal of a lifetime, only a move as sharp and precise as the shot of an arrow can bestow victory on either one of the contenders.

In the conduct of their intricate affairs, Adonsky and Assam Kassani were like two accomplished chess players with the outcome of the encounter dependent on a surprise opening move. Adonsky was now armed with just such an unexpected move. He had contrived the sickness of his friend Assam, then sent Herr Wolff to him. For fifteen years he had been insisting to Assam Kassani that Herr Wolff was the finest doctor in Palestine. It was now time for the crushing blow. Adonsky knew of Assam Kassani's hatred for his offspring who had chosen to live at a distance, those perfumed members of his clan who whispered in French and used his fortune to support a dissolute life.

And so it happened that while Adonsky was at Assam Kassani's bedside studying the ins and outs of the transaction through which he had just acquired eight thousand *dunams* at a bargain price—a rate far lower than he had ever paid, bypassing, with a pretense of indifference, such matters as authorization by the consulates empowering land purchases, as well as the question of deeds with three validating signatures—Assam Kassani lay muttering to himself: Fate is dealing unjustly with me; death is overtaking the wrong man and at the wrong time. Adonsky will profit, but my scoundrels will weep. He laughed to himself but immediately reconsidered. Ah, accursed and dreadful death, he whispered, with pathos appropriate to such a moment. Assam Kassani was, no doubt, bargaining with himself in the fretful manner characteristic of the rich and spoiled who tend to view their approaching death as personal vengeance rather than inexorable fate. He was enraged by the timing. Why now, of all times? And why me in particular? Over there, near the mosque, sits a man about a hundred years old—toothless, trembling, ugly, filthy. He sleeps in the street, lives on scraps, does nothing, adds nothing, is of no use to anyone. After all I have accomplished, after all I have done—why should I die at this early age? What does God gain letting Ahmad Ishohi (that wretched old man) live while requiring Assam Kassani to die? Why, that very spot where the old man lies was restored with my funds.... Which of us has contributed more to the Arab people and to Islam? Ishohi or I?

Adonsky took leave of Kassani and decided to send Shlomzion to see him. He ordered her carriage along with the Arab driver and sent them on their way. Somewhat later, when the powerful remedies provided by Herr Wolff began to produce a fog which was perhaps related to metaphysical concerns, or perhaps the effect of simple fatigue, Assam Kassani began seeing amorphous gray clouds floating about. Through his closed eyelids he saw cities he had never visited, a sea whose shore he had never walked, flowers in a crimson field. Never in the course of his long eventful life had Assam Kassani picked flowers.

It was an autumn day, awesome and glorious, when Shlomzion rode in her carriage to visit Assam Kassani. She carried a bouquet in her hand, the gift of Adonsky and his wife. Adonsky meant for her to bring pleasure to Kassani in his final hours. He would no doubt say (Adonsky mused): Ah, flowers, to place on a grave, as the Jews do. I sold your father a cemetery and now you mean to bury me there? No, I want a Muslim cemetery, without flowers, Shlomzion, with epitaphs to the Prophet.

It didn't occur to poor Assam Kassani that he would be buried in a distant cemetery, near the Yarkon River, in the empty sands beside the grave of the Sheikh. Nor did he know that one day a magnificent hotel would be erected on that site and that the grave of this redeemer of our country's lands would then be moved; that the name of Assam Kassani would be erased, leaving no trace or memory. This ironic fact was of no interest to Shlomzion. Nor would it ever interest her. When I told her they had moved Assam Kassani's grave and built the Hilton in its place, she said, in her private hospital in north Tel Aviv: So what? When you were born, they buried a bottle in your grandmother's house. Whose bottle do you suppose it was? Your mother's? It was given to me by Mr. Svirdoff himself. Your mother had asked: Can I keep it for a day? I gave it to her. So what do you think they did? They put a message in it and buried it under the house. Did your mother return the bottle to me? Why are you so concerned about a dead Arab? Those are his grandchildren who steal across the border to bomb our northern settlements! Right?

Nor did Shlomzion worry about Herr Wolff. At that very moment he was on his way to Adonsky to get the emerald that had been promised him. Immediately thereafter he had a rendezvous in a small café with the sultry commander of Caesarea, who had been waiting tensely for his carrier pigeons to bring secret information relating to an imminent attack on southern Syria by English rebels and their Jewish allies. Herr Wolff sold him the gem and thereupon bought the car of Wagner, the German whose factory was about to be demolished by five cannon shells; after this he would write a letter filled with secrets to the Kaiser, telling how the Jews betray the Arabs, the Arabs betray the Jews, asserting that the Germans could take over quietly and peacefully. Should they so desire.

Shlomzion's sorrow during her visit with Assam will be measured and intelligent. He will understand her. She will not weep, nor will she be verbose. She will be appropriately sad, full of flowers, beauty, chill. He will know to appreciate her visit, though it is clear to him who sent her and why. Assam Kassani will no doubt think: In human relations pretense is forbidden—a view shared by Adonsky and Shlomzion. One must acknowledge hate and envy, yet behave according to the rules of the game. In this case, everyone has followed the rules, Assam will assure himself, focusing on the gates of paradise and the birds floating through his murky mind.

11

It was an enchanted autumn day: the sky was blue and light as gauze; the silence like a concentration of feathers; the sea still, without a ripple. The road was lined with citrus groves, cactus hedges, jasmine and oleander bushes whose scent merged with mint and acacia. The limbs of the trees were sharply defined, as if bathed by a meticulous mother, appearing at once brash and disciplined. Shlomzion was in the carriage, wearing a filmy white dress, its collar like small banners, a fine lace hat perched on her head, white gloves in hand. She held a bouquet wrapped in rustling paper. When Shlomzion spied the ship peering over the horizon and approaching the shore slowly, she asked her driver to stop. After a while, masts, flags, portholes, cannons were visible; against the backdrop of smooth sea, they had a relaxed and affable air, molded in water, dipped in sky that skimmed the water cautiously. Nonetheless, the scene alarmed Shlomzion and affected her with a sensation of inexplicable violence. She clasped the bouquet to her throbbing heart; her hands pressed the roses, their thorns prickling her and flooding her with sudden joy. She longed to hunt animals in the jungle, to be bound at the stake in a legendary tale, to cry, to explode. Something menacing erupted within her all at once, despite the placid innocence, and the day, more enchanting than any she recalled. Thin white smoke curled upward from the ship, barely touching the flocks of birds that circled the sky. Shlomzion, whose face was delicate, whose dark eyes were set in violet pits, watched with considerable indignation while small waves, like soda bubbles, licked the clean bathed sand.

In the stillness, Shlomzion spotted several figures moving stealthily, a rush of activity the nature of which she could not discern. Horses galloped in the distance, sending up dust that trailed like chimney smoke into the silence enclosed in sweetness. She thought at first that the smoke was unreal, perceiving it from her distant perspective like a large curtain with lions and tigers drawn on it. She, Shlomzion, was a five-year-old in a fetching dress, holding a toy cannon, shooting at a pretend enemy, about to be photographed against a jungle backdrop for the sake of eternity—a sweet curly-haired child in Abu-Hamdi's studio on Bustrus Street. Two anchors were cast into the water. Then, in a flash, a white rowboat was lowered into the sea. Several figures, one of them in gleaming white, stood erect in the boat while it was lowered by a crane. When no longer connected to the larger vessel, it began making its way toward the shore. One long whistle and two shorter ones pierced the air. Flags were lowered, others raised in their place. Sailors with spyglasses darted about the deck. The cannons on board were unsheathed and seemed to be aimed at Shlomzion. The barrels were raised slightly, lowered again, then set at the proper level. Only then did this placid scene become concrete, though inherently so all the time, everything advancing rapidly toward a fate perhaps unknown yet gripping. The cloud of dust subsided, the horses having arrived at a point on the shore which was opposite the boat. Several riders could be seen. Three of them advanced toward the water line. From behind, Shlomzion identified Hassan-Bek by his bow-legs and Bha-Aladdin by his elegant coat. The horses recoiled, neighed in alarm and stamped their hooves in the soft sand. Shlomzion's driver, who had remained in place, suddenly began shouting: That's a French warship! Until that moment she was aware only of the distance between the people. She had heard a terrible war was imminent; now she understood how magnificent and noble war could be.

The boat glided over the water like a toy engraved in crystal. The Turks on their snorting horses were gesturing agitatedly, their gaze fixed on the approaching boat. The vessel in the background was engulfed in mist. Bha-Aladdin's back was tense with stolid power, restrained as a taut spring. Shlomzion had never seen such physical intensity. She was captivated by the charmed opposition between the boat gliding over water (like the music of Swan Lake when she was in Carlsbad with her father the previous summer) and the taut violent back of Bha-Aladdin. Savagery versus delicacy, she thought, which is just as it ought to be.

This definition brought her to a state of intense ecstasy, though she didn't give herself a precise account of her intent. Shlomzion was captivated or subdued, as she explained to herself, by the splendor and majesty, perhaps even the despair of the Turk, the calm about to erupt. She herself was merely a sublime theatrical device, consisting of clever stage effects, lights, curtain, backdrop. Bha-Aladdin didn't match the image of a revered Jewish watchman, hero of countless tales related by the teacher Nahumi along with folk-dance lessons and songs of the land; nor did he suggest a Jewish youth rejecting religion to mount a horse, slinging a gun over his shoulder and going out to be built and rebuilt in the hills of Galilee, declaring: He who breaks fences will be stung by a serpent. The costume was identical—the mustache, the strained back—but there were differences it was hard for her to articulate between the images idealized by Nahumi and that of Bha-Aladdin. Bha-Aladdin was an enemy revered by cannons aimed at the shore in a grandiose game with each side recognizing the opponent's strength, each enemy yearning for its counterpart. She was recalling the play of the swans in Carlsbad, the strange old man in a leather suit and Tyrolean hat who bowed to her, turned pale and proclaimed: Your eternal servant, Fräulein! That night he expired, leaving her name scrawled on a yellowed sheet of paper found beside his bed in a dingy room. She went to the funeral, watched her aged admirer lowered into the grave; she was unable to mourn him. Swans and enmity, she thought to herself, aroused once again by words she had never used before. Peace and snorting horses . . . Mustaches, all the more striking on figures in white, as if etched in butter, in a crystal boat, moving toward stilted rage. Flocks of birds continued to perform their dazzling stunts in the bright sky, and for the first time in her life, perhaps the last as well, Shlomzion was enthralled by something monumental outside of herself, something beautiful etched in marble that could not exist otherwise, totally unadulterated. She may have dimly thought that this moment in which she was taking part, dressed in white, bouquet in hand, was the crucial one, an event after which nothing would be as it had been before. The entire century was, perhaps, being sealed, or the millennium. From here on the world would be a reflection of what she and her father had always pictured, though others were incapable of sharing their vision. It could be that there no longer was, nor would there be again, any conflict in the world. She, Shlomzion, was the final challenge. And she had just demolished her enemies, unto the last one.

Now, more than ever, she detested her school friends, the shouts and whispers in the night, the sentimental songs. At the same time she adored this desperate, scarred land more than she could admit. She measured the land in units of dream and orchard, Turkish officials and German engineers, distinguished Jews coming to construct dream castles there. Remembering Simha, the handsome teacher who rode a donkey to the girls' school at Neve-Zedek, she arrived at a decisive thought, an awareness of Simha's son Nehemiah, whom she had met twice, to whom she had never before devoted a moment's attention. Now, faced with the rigid back of Bha-Aladdin, with the great moment about to be unleashed as the boat advanced at a relaxed, leisurely pace, she was gripped by thoughts of Nehemiah, her life, her brazen love for him, his ecstatic love for her, mystical to the point of innocence, absolute and ultimate. It was as if her entire future unfolded in that moment.

Shlomzion had met Nehemiah twice. Once, on Rehov Herzl, a street regarded by those who lived on it as singular in Jewish history, a crossroads joining two thousand years of exile with Israel's ancient glory. This metahistorical junction bustled with humanity on that particular day. Students going to and from the Gymnasia greeted each other. There were several one- and two-story buildings on the street that seemed bemused by the excitement. Simha and his son Nehemiah were rushing off somewhere. Nehemiah was seventeen at the time, seventeen times two thousand years of resurgence. But he looked to her then, as now, like a mere seventeen. Here comes Queen Shlomzion with Nebuchadnezzar, King of Assyria, Nehemiah had said. Adonsky remarked to her: Simha's son is very much like his father, dreaming of the hole in an Egyptian coin. Without faith in the land there is no faith in the Jewish people. Zionist thinkers will have streets named for them, but our people will be redeemed because of those who see what surrounds the hole in the coin; Simha isn't even worthy of the hole.

She didn't think about this encounter, perhaps even forgot it.

Another time they met in the courtyard of the Gymnasia. He grinned at her and said: Queen Shlomzion, come to the beach with me. We'll study sandology, my pretty one—"for the voice of the turtle is heard in the land!"

She turned away and he was faced with the most beautiful back in Tel Aviv (ever).

She now realized that Nehemiah loved her to distraction. His image assumed substance, became deeply vital. He was her total life and she was his. He would be husband to her, father of her children, sire of her grandchildren. She would shield him with her body, rescue him from the mad dream world of the first Hebrew Gymnasia in two thousand years.

She was betrothed to him on the limestone rock of Jaffa's shore, watching the approach of the boat.

The silence was as yet unbroken; everything remained potential. The guns were aimed at Shlomzion. She was considering: Flowers for Assam Kassani? Flowers for the grave in which my youth will be buried, for I am soon to be married!

For the first time in her life, Shlomzion was overcome by pity, self-pity, pity for Nehemiah, the Turkish officers, the moment that would never be retrieved.

All that would ever be was included in this moment. Henceforth, she knew, she would no longer grow, change, depend on any event. All of her future moments were being created, inspired, by this brief instant.

The tension between the approaching boat and the rigid back of Bha-Aladdin, most cruel of all the rulers of the land, was distinct from her, an equivalent of her love. She studied the boat, the man in his gleaming white uniform and colorful hat holding a flag. He didn't stir. Framed by the boat's graceful progress through the silky waves, his posture was proud. When the boat touched the sand, two oarsmen leaped out, waited for the young officer to disembark and reach the shore, saluted, then pulled the boat after them. The officer moved in a measured pace, halted, blinked in the blinding sun, passed the flag to one of the rowers, who was standing at attention, saluted and took an at-ease position. The officer approached the Turks, who were still on horseback. They hesitated, returning his salute with a pretense of indifference.

Not a single word had been said as yet. Still, Shlomzion sensed that they, too, those mighty ones, Bha-Aladdin the Great and bow-legged Hassan-Bek, were enthralled by the unreal and perplexing scene. Her driver wailed and repressed the sound with his hairy hand. Shlomzion detested him for clouding the wondrous moment, for failing to hear the music, the rustle of the curtain about to fall, as it had fallen in the small theatre in Carlsbad.

The young officer didn't hear the wail of the driver, whose face was still hidden in his hands. He drew a scroll of paper, or perhaps parchment, from his belt and handed it to Bha-Aladdin, murmuring French words.

Bha-Aladdin didn't understand.

One of the Turks approached from behind, took the scroll and read it aloud. Bha-Aladdin listened attentively to the graceful ring of the French, then to the metallic translation. The translator read French fluently, with showy pathos, whereas the Turkish sounded shabby. The rowers were still posted beside the strip of water, the sun beating down on their heads.

The letter conveyed a request from the captain of the French ship in the name of the French Admiralty, as well as the French government and its military chief, that he be granted singular permission by the commander of Jaffa to fire five cannon shells at the factory of Wagner, the German, situated in the dunes of Jaffa. The Turk paused a minute, pointed to a spot directly behind Shlomzion and resumed reading: Thus the captain requests, in the names of the aforementioned, that said proposal be seriously considered and suggests that said act be appropriately compensated. The most logical recompense, the Turk read, continuing to translate, would call upon the Turks to fire five shots at the ship immediately after it fires at the factory. The French further request that said shots, if they are indeed to be fired, be delayed until after they raise anchor.

At this point the Turk stepped back and Bha-Aladdin and Hassan-Bek, along with two senior officers, began considering the proposal and gesturing agitatedly.

Shlomzion, taut and attentive, blazed with the fire of muted passion. She knew there were no cannons in Jaffa, nor was there anyone to fire them. She laughed to herself (though she didn't know how to laugh at all) as she watched the Turks nod, the French officer salute. As soon as the salute was returned, the two rowers signaled their ship. On deck, flags were raised and lowered. Sailors darted to and fro studying the shore through spyglasses. Watching Bha-Aladdin, Shlomzion saw his tension diminish, his back relax. He saluted the French officer with grace and decided joy, like a boy engaged in a thrilling game. In the background, the ship looked so delightful and decadent that Shlomzion plucked a flower from her bouquet and flung it wildly toward her driver, who continued to tremble and moan into his hand.

Bha-Aladdin dismounted. The officer approached and kissed him on both cheeks. Bha-Aladdin seemed alarmed, rubbed his cheek in dismay and bestowed wild kisses on the thin fragile officer. He was followed by Hassan-Bek, short, bow-legged and plump, with a splendid mustache. Hassan-Bek responded to the officer's salute with a shower of impassioned kisses. The anxious officer, on the verge of losing his balance, managed to maintain a tense and official smile. From a distance Shlomzion noted mute distress masked by smiles. She observed the pathos of the scene as the fragile French officer was kissed by three wild Turks in a rush of childish delight. The officer seemed to her like the sublime fusion of a delicate flower with a wind-up doll. The vigor, and even more important, the absoluteness of his actions, seemed imprinted in his body. He, nonetheless, appeared innocent, childlike, amiable and somewhat dull, as if following a score composed long ago by someone remote and long since vanished. It is a tradition, she explained to herself, tradition *française*, her attention shifting to pianos, music teachers, tender strangers in dim rooms. *Bonjour*, Monsieur Mahluf, and *bonsoir*, Monsieur Abdul-Hamid . . . The fragrance of perfume, vague melancholy, a lump of sugar in thin china cups, afternoon tea in the cool breeze as evening descends.

The Turks, excited by this momentous yet entertaining event, bestowed endless kisses on the officer, who became more and more pale, though the smile remained fixed on his face. Finally, taking the flag from one of the rowers, the officer saluted the flag as well as the Turks, then signaled his men. He waited for them to push the boat into the water, boarded it and stood at attention, holding the flag high. The small boat made its way toward the ship's twinkling silver lights.

The Turks hesitated, gazing with wonder at the menacing purity. Then they turned and began galloping speedily toward the town. Pillars of dust and sand covered the horizon. The driver pressed Shlomzion. She dismissed him scornfully. He looked at her, baffled, shrugged his shoulders, tied the horses to a tree and slipped away to the shelter of some ruins in a nearby grove of palm trees. Only the smoke of his cigarette could be discerned trailing through the broken window, which he tried to stuff with crumbling limestone.

Shlomzion stood facing the sea in a white bridal dress, bouquet in hand. She was consumed with happiness, a sensation somewhere between cruel triumphant wonder and absolute submission.

The sound of horses' hooves . . . Shlomzion, at this moment, was arranging her marriage to Nehemiah, fashioning her days, rearing her children, all without an excess of elation. Everything was foreseen yet surprising. Her driver shouted, but she didn't hear. On the hill, behind her, near the factory of Wagner, the German, there was a rush of activity. Someone was starting a car. A woman's shriek was heard and the long continuous wail of a dog. Shlomzion didn't look back, nor did she turn even when she heard Wagner's car pass on the dirt road.

Wagner's car was the only one in Jaffa. Children threw rocks at it; veiled women cursed it and muttered imprecations to protect them from the evil eye. Shlomzion responded to the scent of fear that issued from the car. She knew, without turning, that Mr. Wagner was driving, the perennial sun hat on his head, a cigar in his mouth, his elegantly dressed ladies urging him on. She knew that neither they nor anyone else (with the possible exception of Bha-Aladdin) could grasp this exquisite moment. They miss the high points of life, she once told Nahumi. They live, they die unacquainted with the great moments. I remember being born, when, how and where. What's more, I will be awake when I die. When the five shots were fired, I was there. It was the middle of my life, its very midst; I observed that moment from within and without.

Aunt Shlomit used to say, over a fragrant cup of coffee: She won't miss it, that's clear! She'll watch her own death like a Bette Davis movie, arriving at the gates of heaven or hell in colorful gift-wrap, a present from herself to herself. She will teach God compassion. His brutality will seem trivial to her. Shlomzion the Great has been cruising through life in a glass-bottomed boat, floating through the sewage, says Aunt Shlomit. She knows what everything costs; she sniffs evil from afar. . . . Did you know she collected bags full of pennies? She skimped and bargained and accumulated a fortune. When Nehemiah died, she dragged the pennies on her back to the bank. . . . Did you know how much change she accumulated in thirty-five years, not to mention the period when she was the wife of an ambassador in Paris and London and dined with the Graf Pototzky?

How much? (In our family rhetorical questions are a sign of familiarity.)

She had 156,000 lirot. All in pennies!

Aunt Shlomit drank her coffee with great involvement.

Shlomzion, who did not know what Aunt Shlomit would say about her in years to come, stood on the hill ablaze with passion, watching as the cannons were moved into position: raised, lowered, focused. Red-and-black flags did a whirling dance on the tall masts. She smiled in embarrassment and pleasure. The flowers clung to her dress. And so Shlomzion felt the five cannon shots flash through her hair, like electric shocks, at intervals of a minute or two, and the explosion, echoing nearby, gripped her while it shocked and humiliated the pedestrian world all around her. The intervals between the shots were marked by silence. The world held its breath and the massive explosions were punctuated by the wails of her driver in his shelter. Birds circled in astonished sorrow. Two shells hit the factory, three exploded near it. Several rounds of gunshot were heard. The birds resumed their graceful motion. The sea remained silent. The ship lifted anchor and turned its prow to the shore. A moment of treachery and tension. Shlomzion knew she would not be shot at. Smoke trailed from the ship as flags were raised and lowered on its deserted deck.

Ten minutes of suspense filled with malice. Total stillness. Not even a horse stirred. A few shots were heard. A trail of smoke from Wagner's factory. A car horn, answered by a dog's wail, echoed in the distance. The horses snorted and stopped in their tracks. Shlomzion's driver smoked one cigarette after another. Then the French ship blew its horn, emitting a tone of disdain disguised as dismay, circled and turned toward the horizon.

A flight of birds followed, infatuated with the smoke and the beauty of the masts, circling madly, arranging itself in striking ballet formation, making bold and imaginative patterns. The smoke soared higher and higher. The image of the slim officer in white, a delicate flower with the manner of a wind-up doll, was imprinted on Shlomzion's field of vision only to merge with the edict of silence.

12

Shlomzion the Great understood the moment and celebrated it. She said to me once: I honored that moment, but Abu-Naim hid away in the ruins!

Her son Arty said to me: She pitied no one. . . . He didn't believe there were no casualties, and even Wagner's factory was only partially destroyed.

Now, too, in the private hospital in north Tel Aviv, on days when she forgets everything, she doesn't forget the instant when the shells flashed gloriously through her hair. The Nazi factory was demolished, she says. They're Nazis even before they are born.

She told Mother Shlomzion how she gave birth to herself at that moment and took Nehemiah to be her husband.

Little Mother Shlomzion corrects her: You were married to him.

It was I who took him! she retorts angrily. Fool! I say I took him and I know the difference.

Ah, says Little Mother Shlomzion.

And then I thought about the words *to conceive*, Shlomzion the Great continues.

Little Mother Shlomzion blushes.

Don't make a face, Shlomzion the Great says to Little Mother Shlomzion in the bright hospital room. Because you don't have much face left. And stop envying me. It's not my fault you look the way you do, or that doctors fall desperately in love with me. They've always fallen in love with me—what can I do? Did anyone ever claim that God is fair, that He follows the rules? It wasn't easy to make a match for you! By the way, how is your poor Naftali?

He died three years ago, Mother Shlomzion offers quietly.

No tragedy, says Shlomzion the Great. Not for him, for you, for any of us. You'll find someone else. At your age men want money, not looks, and after all, you do have money. You can surely find someone at Nahumi's. They get together there on Friday nights to share chicken soup and memories. There's an ample supply of widowers there. You have money and an apartment, so what's the problem? It won't be hard.

This was the day when Aunt Shlomzion the Great decided that Mother was secretly married to a young man but was afraid to bring him to the hospital lest he, too, fall in love with her. Bring him here, she said, I'll make myself as ugly as you. I won't tell him about the rugs and silver you stole from me.

Once, when I came to visit her, she whispered: Did you know your mother's young husband was here and tried . . . you know what? Exactly like your grandfather. Did you know your grandfather tried, too? Don't be surprised. He tried to make out with everyone. Right after I was married to Nehemiah, he came one night and tried. Tell me, she said, your mother's new husband— is he older than you?

No, I said. He's younger. He's in twelfth grade, a Communist, one-eyed and half Jewish. He was convicted of treason. He killed his mother, more than once. He is involved in a plot to overthrow the government. He is a fashion designer, speaks only English and Arabic. He wasn't even circumcised.

She stared at me a long interval: How do you know he wasn't circumcised? You and your mother discuss that sort of thing? He's my adopted son, I said. I almost gave birth to him. What a family, she said. You, Aunt Shlomit and your mother! That's right, I said.
During this period, she said to Mother: You come here thinking you'll get something? I did, in fact, think about the words *"to conceive,"* and I did make Nehemiah my husband. You pretend to be my husband's sister and come here for charity. It won't get you anywhere. . . . You look terrible, she added. You look tired, tired from all that stealing. You won't be able to get at my keys anymore. My doctors are protecting me!
Mother was silent.
I said "to conceive," Aunt Shlomzion the Great repeated.
I heard you, said Little Mother Shlomzion, tormented yet meaning well.
Aunt Shlomzion the Great lay in her bed grandly, looking out at the grim sky. Rain was about to fall. I conceived, she said, in and of myself!
She always had a rare talent for words, I remarked. Old Nahumi corrected me: Had, has and will have—an almost divine talent! We cherish our own henchmen, he added sadly. Those who humiliate us and pierce us with daggers.
I conceived in and of myself!
Little Mother Shlomzion repeated this phrase (which I later repeated to old Nahumi). She tried pitying Shlomzion the Great, wondering how she arrived at these humane and civil words midst drawn swords.
I left Mother's house. It was Saturday night. Rain was falling. I considered: Why not write about Aunt Shlomzion? I went to Rothschild Boulevard. Adonsky's buildings are so vacant at night, among thickly twined trees with violet crowns. A boulevard of parked cars. I arrived at Shlomzion's house. It was quiet, enveloped in bougainvillaea. In the courtyard was the tree my uncle had planted forty-five years back when he worked for Aronson in Zichron Yaakov. All around was silence. The secretaries

in short dresses who typed letters in triplicate on rented machines were now dancing in night spots, strolling, lying in warm beds with or without, watching suspense movies on TV. I stole into the yard. Why was I so afraid? I am overcome with terror every time I pass through that large creaky gate. The yard smelled of damp grass that grew wild and untended. I studied the rear wall of the house and found traces of the dog house that was there thirty years ago. I waited. Would Rex leap out to greet me, sniff my pants craving love? In this yard Arpahshad showed me pictures of a nude girl and boy in a room filled with old furniture in Cairo. Shlomzion appeared suddenly, her face severe and full of contempt. She said to her son: If you do that with your hands, you won't have anything left to make peepee with! Arpahshad gazed at her with wild animosity, as if he had lost the last shred of hope. Later he took the dress Shlomzion had just brought home from Mrs. Virsovsky, the dressmaker, after a final fitting, and flung it into Rex's dog house.

My cousin spread the dress on the floor, placed two juicy bones on top of it and beckoned to his beloved dog. The frightened animal stood trembling, his tongue dripping saliva, and refused to partake of the feast. My cousin commanded: Go Rex, go. Get a move on, you old motherfucker! Poor Arpahshad was muttering repeated imprecations, stammering, drawing out each syllable: mmmothththther-ffffuck-errrr. The dog waited patiently for the end of the phrase. My cousin, flushed with excitement, got down on all fours. He was wearing three-quarter pants, which had become the mark of his élite school (Gymnasia Herzlia) and of Tel Aviv's golden boys, a Betty Grable medallion, shirt sleeves rolled to the elbow. He licked the bones; then the dog began to growl. He was jealous and began whining furiously. My cousin loved Rex more than any creature in the world, so much so that Aunt Shlomzion didn't allow the dog in the house. Sometimes, unbeknownst to Shlomzion, my cousin would spend the night with Rex in the dog house. It was during World War II, when my uncle drove around in a Model T Ford, when the people on Rothschild Boulevard were selling land to the British, building their army camps and cheating in the interest of patriotism. In those golden days Arpahshad used to sleep with Rex, especially in summer. There were blackouts; great quantities of sour cream were consumed; many rounds of tennis were played with the English; my uncle's inventions advanced the Allied cause. Shlomzion the Great drank tea in thin china cups during this period and chided Little Mother Shlomzion: Your son Aminadav climbs trees, rips his pants, associates with Communists in the immigrant camps, goes off to build new settlements in the north where they'll soon be showering in the nude and making babies. But Arpahshad plays tennis, photographs natural-looking girls in Jaffa, goes to parties with young ladies from good homes! When in the world will your son become a man?

Rex finally made the leap. He first licked my cousin, greedily, then began devouring the bones. He hid one bone under the dress, burrowed until he tore a large hole in it; he tucked another bone away under the dress while devouring the first one; without concluding this course, he retrieved the hidden bone and began digging into it. He switched bones at a feverish pace, always leaving one under the dress, which began to look more like a strainer than an article of clothing. The holes in the garment brought glee to Arpahshad's despondent eyes.

At this point Shlomzion the Great burst onto the scene. She remained silent for a moment, glaring at her son with a sort of mute enmity. Then she looked at me. She behaved like a trained animal. Her outrage was restrained and measured. She fixed her gaze on her son. His knees were trembling. The dog retreated to a corner and began to whine, then to bark. Aunt Shlomzion did not even look his way. He curled up and tried to press close to my cousin, but Arpahshad moved away. Then Rex made the mistake of his brief lifetime. He moved toward Shlomzion in an effort to redeem himself. He tried to lick her leg. My cousin emitted a frantic whistle.

Aunt Shlomzion seized the stick that was used to lock the shed and struck Rex. One sharp blow, like the blow of a samurai; then she vanished.

The blow was crushing.

My cousin spit blood, as if he had been struck. His mouth was dry and blood spouted from it. I hurried away. Aunt Shlomzion stopped me at the front door: Go through the yard, she said. No one invited you. You might as well leave like the hired help.

From that day on Rex whined constantly. He was chained whenever my cousin left for school. Shlomzion used to pour cold water on him and leave his food just beyond the range of his chain, so he could see it but not reach it. In the evening my cousin would bring him food.

When Arpahshad went on a class trip and was away for five days, Nehemiah brought Rex food on the sly. Rex didn't touch the food. He managed to stretch his chain so he could reach Arpahshad's bicycle. He lay there for five days without stirring, and died beside the bicycle two hours before my cousin returned from his trip.

When he got back, exhausted and sunburned, Arpahshad saw Rex sprawled beside the bicycle. He bent down to pet him. Rex was still warm. His face was not distorted, as if he had anticipated peace and achieved it.

My cousin sat beside the dead dog, his knapsack on his back, his face parched, and moaned, stammering and drawing out the first two letters of the dead dog's name interminably.

The dog house is no longer there. There are little foxes in the melancholy houses of the crumbling city that flees northward lamenting the sweet and handsome houses of Tel Aviv's innocent founders. I want to write about Aunt Shlomzion the Great from deep within the drama of Tel Aviv's builders, among structures that resemble the palaces of cardboard princes now vacant and deflated. She created a son whose light is extinct. Created a son. Created. Later, in the process of creation, she may have quenched his light. He stammers, is riddled with anxiety, has become a protector of stray souls, though his life is held together with safety pins and he himself is on the verge of collapse. I wonder what motivates Aunt Shlomzion—Sound and fury, said Macbeth. I am sitting in the yard. The rains are over and gone.

Pain appears in our land. The dog houses are gone, the little foxes are gone. The houses crumble in tired dignity, beggar-kings on new streets ruled by formica potentates. The élite of Tel Aviv lived here once. Spider webs and rust remain. Still, pride and faded grandeur, discreet gentility, persist, along with secretaries in short dresses typing letters in triplicate to nonexistent clients. A tantalizing smell rich with remembrance of thin smoke, damp grass and roasted coffee fills the yard. The sharp odor of benzene from the avenue merges with the fragrance of the bougainvillaea and ivy, reminding me of Nehemiah. He used to spend Saturday afternoons in the yard, in a lounge chair, reading. I think of poor Rex, the wounded look in his eyes. No man ever looked at me as Rex did when Shlomzion struck him. Nehemiah's glasses . . . The blow . . . My cousin stammering his dog's name. Shlomzion says to Little Mother Shlomzion: I conceived in and of myself. I understand; I suddenly understand. I speculate: Until that enchanted day when five shells were fired by the French boat, Shlomzion did not consciously connect those sweet and terrifying tales about the Jaffa sands with Dr. Hissin, in his white hat, riding through the night on horseback to bring a Hebrew baby into the world. But all things fused then; she felt the astonishment of defeat along with great triumph. She was married to Nehemiah and, what's more, she married him though he still knew nothing of this. She pressed her entire life into a ball, cradled it in her hand; life and death compressed together, a single essence suggesting symmetry in which the seed contains the tree and the tree contains the seed. Her pronouncement that she had conceived in and of herself took on clear significance. To avert any further change, to be carved in final form within the immutable metamorphoses of life, to be reborn in a mold identical to the one already assumed, she gave birth to herself. To be mistress, to hold a course in the turbulent waters, to represent eternity on the head of a pin. This was my understanding there in the yard overgrown with weeds and wild grasses. A young woman in a filmy white dress confronting the most glorious moment of her life. I wanted to go inside, to touch the walls, look

13

Throughout the Great War, Shlomzion lived with a sensation of rarefied terror. People were dying by the thousands. Children disappeared into the dunes and were felled by typhus. A young neighbor girl was sold to a German officer with a monocle. Jews who didn't have Ottoman citizenship were expelled from the country. The Arabs said: Capitulation is at hand—death to the Jews. Ships sank to the bottom of a placid sea covered with gentle ripples. People lived on bulghur and grasses. Cripples on crutches dragged weapons for the Turkish Army. Barefoot soldiers, wrapped in rags, carried heavy packs down the beach, cut trees to provide fuel for trains heading south never to return. Engines captured en route to the front, whose precise location was unknown, sent an anguished roar into the night. Nehemiah was drafted. At first he donned the uniform of a Turkish officer and was sent to a military school. Then he was transferred to the infantry to carry munitions. Many of his friends died from malaria and typhus. My Grandfather Simha hid in a garret and died there. When the residents of Tel Aviv were evacuated to Kfar

Saba and Petah Tikva, Adonsky was allowed to remain in Jaffa. Shlomzion sat at the window overlooking the sea. The winters were difficult, the summers hot and misty, the mites prolific. She saw neither the fires being lit throughout the countryside to ward off locusts nor the famine. Her vision was dominated by the image of the French officer. Processions of chained Jews passed her house. They were being whipped by a Turk with a mustache. She didn't notice any of this, being preoccupied with her Frenchman strolling through his private Tuileries Gardens where handsome trees shed leaves in her honor and fine sculpture blocked the wind with frozen grace. She saw glorious cannon fire pierce the halo that ringed her head. When the hungry barefoot orchestra began playing at the foot of her terrace, Shlomzion watched Antoine embrace Nehemiah, planting kisses on both his cheeks. The orchestra played while Adonsky received little Jamal-Pasha and his band of officers. When Jamal-Pasha waved his hand, they stopped playing and the performers fell to the ground. A Turkish soldier flung them a crust of bread. They crawled, on all fours, to taste the dried-out crust. Then they played again, entertaining Adonsky and his guests, who were feasting on roast veal in piquant sauce. Shlomzion refused to take note of them, refused to believe they existed. Even when Nehemiah appeared, exhausted and tattered, seeking refuge in her house, recounting tales of combat, hunger, brutality, she insisted that the horror of wars tends to be exaggerated, that war is not as everyone describes it.

She has endured many wars since that one. World War I lasted four years. It was followed by the riots of '21, during which Abner was wounded on the Jaffa-Tel Aviv line and Asaf Kusinetsky's leg was amputated on Adonsky's kitchen table by the light of a lantern (without Adonsky's knowledge). There were riots again in '29, when Nehemiah designed bombs for the Haganah and went out to defend Tel Aviv armed with an old revolver. Aunt Shlomzion the Great stood before the round mirror inherited from her mother trying on clothes, sly indifference on her face, the smile of a tired God. More riots in '36, designated by the Arabs as revolution. Buses were attacked. There were daily death notices. They began burying youngsters in the new burial grounds in Nahlat Yitzhak—no one knew where they were from or why they had died. School friends founded new settlements in the dark of the night so the remedy would precede the blow. Then came World War II, when the house opposite Shlomzion's was destroyed by a misguided Italian bomb. And the War of Independence, the Sinai War, the Six-Day War, the War of Attrition, the Yom Kippur War. There were distant wars in remote places brought to her via television, with blood, pain, much anguish and hunger. Still, during all those years, Shlomzion the Great continued to regard war as a stylized enterprise, dramatized by kisses on the cheek, involving murder, but conducted according to proper rules with surprise cannon fire gliding through her hair. To her war was like life itself: impossible to comprehend yet indispensable. Was it not like chivalry with its elements of glory and malice? That enchanted memory of violin music on the beach as the five shots streaked through her hair toward the factory of Wagner, the German, became a barrier on her threshold, shielding her from distress so that life's terrors never once touched her.

Cannon fire in her hair. The Turks have stopped shooting. The ship moves toward the horizon. Shlomzion, happy beyond anything she has ever experienced, is paying a final visit to Assam Kassani. On the way, after the boat was out of sight and the driver emerged from his shelter, she met Vladya Abramsky, who, years later, would become a justice of the peace in Tel Aviv, known as Abrams. He was picking autumn flowers and so absorbed in gathering them and arranging them to dry on special absorbent sheets that he heard neither the cannon shell nor the horses' hooves nor the Turkish gunfire. He was not aware that an era had ended. He didn't even notice Mr. Wagner driving past in the car close to where he stood engrossed in lavender squill, splendid as a king, as he explained to Shlomzion's intense astonishment. Her radiant happiness was so effusive that even the scent of the flowers did not shield him. Entranced by the glorious scene unfolding before him, he tipped his hat and greeted Shlomzion. She said: What a fine day. He answered: Yes, an enchanted day—such air, such flowers. She said: And the boat! He asked: What boat? She said: The shells. He said: The sea shells? She descended from her carriage and told him, wrapped in infinite joy and yearning for herself, that one day she would reward him for his courtly manner. All his life Abrams cherished the jubilant image of Shlomzion in her gauzy white dress, bouquet in hand, totally pure. Whenever she was criticized, he would say: But she is so innocent and marvelous; when I saw her in the orchard, she was delicate and transparent, the essence of beauty and naïveté.

He alone, in all of Jaffa, failed to hear the shells. And so Shlomzion entrusted him with the key to her mysterious finances. Abrams is now very sick, in a hospital in Raanana, half paralyzed. He sits in a wheelchair and is fed by a young nurse, who listens to Mickey Mirth on the radio and laughs at his jokes. Abrams never married. He has no children or relatives. The key is in his hand, though he doesn't know why he was favored. He thinks: Shlomzion, Nehemiah's wife, mother of Wondrous-Counsel-Prince of Peace . . . and remembers a young girl beaming with joy.

She said to me once: He is a very fine man, respects beauty, sends criminals to jail and dries flowers. He doesn't even remember that they are locked in there. He believes in law, she says; in beauty, in rules. Her voice rings with excitement, the identical quality with which she pours tea from a fine lavender urn into delicate cups or, for that matter, the excitement with which she struck Rex.

After Shlomzion took leave of Assam Kassani, she returned to Jaffa. The city was astir with rumors of war. Turkish soldiers were posting draft notices. A long line of young men hoping to get Ottoman citizenship stretched from the post office as far as the eye could see. She went home, changed her clothes and went to Tel Aviv to the home of Nahumi, the teacher, on Lilienblum Street, for lessons in folk dancing and new-old songs. Nahumi was pleased to see her. He danced (for her alone) an old-new Biblical dance which, to several of the daughters of Tel Aviv's most erudite citizens, recalled Jacob's movements when seeking Rachel's hand from Laban, movements characterized by abandon and grace. The girls were excited by this dance which, in Nahumi's opinion, had archaic vitality expressed through gestures containing magical elements. Aunt Shlomzion applauded and, in the process, began thinking of Nehemiah and of her handsome Frenchman, who, at that very moment, was perhaps engaged in some Provençal dance in the company of birds enchanted by his spell, kissing poor cavalry officers in a remote port or firing at German factories somewhere in the world.

After leaving Nahumi's house, hand in hand with Sarah Izmosky, she asked Sarah (on whose behalf she had actually come) if the new-word party was in fact taking place that night at the home of their teacher, Bugrashov. Baffled by Shlomzion's sudden interest, Sarah answered: Yes, it is tonight, and the words being honored are orchestra and cucumber.

That evening Sarah called for her. Adonsky served cherry liqueur and asked after her distinguished father—had he sold the lot they had discussed some time ago? Sarah didn't know the answer. Adonsky, losing interest in the girl, retired to his room. Sarah and Shlomzion went to the home of Bugrashov, their teacher, to welcome the two new words into the covenant of the Hebrew language and to celebrate its miraculous revival. Bugrashov spoke about the power of the word, how we weld worlds by wielding words, old and new; we begin with the word, which was in the beginning, and discover, in the spiritual depths of our people, in its verbal treasure-trove, words to serve our modern needs. The young folks exclaimed: Orchestra, orchestra! Orchestra; from the Latin word chorus. Our orchestra is large. Our orchestra will sing tonight. The national orchestra will sing tonight.

The party was very festive. The word orchestra, it was noted, derived from the Latin, is an appropriate term for a company of performers. Which was well and good until some misguided individual printed chorus in place of orchestra and orchestra in place of chorus. So that in the new Hebrew, what should have been called an orchestra was called a chorus, and what should have been called a chorus was called an orchestra.

To this day Shlomzion the Great says: We are going to hear our great orchestra sing Bach chorales. As far as she is concerned, those she considers *nouveau riche* go to hear the Israel Philharmonic Chorus.

But Shlomzion was not concerned with words just then, not even with wielding the word and dedicating it to share the destiny of Hebrew revived. Despite the cheers of the young men and women, despite their enthusiasm, she remained cool. She was waiting for Nehemiah and he did indeed come. He approached her, summoning all his charm, and said: Welcome, Shlomzion the Beautiful; our sandology has not achieved even the golden ore of an orchestra. He had, in fact, just been listening to the Arabs chant, Death to the Jews, capitulation is at hand, down with the Jewish colony! He was expecting a great war, which he knew would be severe. He, too, was aware that a millennium was at an end.

But, having come to the party to rejoice and forget, he found himself being bound in a sly and fatal troth, a troth of shame and madness, to a woman with five cannon shells streaking through her hair. He didn't understand what was happening. When he approached Shlomzion, a smile danced across his lips. She laughed exquisitely and fixed her broad penetrating gaze on him, her eyes filled with mute yearning. He, poor fellow, blushed. He asked what she was doing in their circle all of a sudden. Her eyes, the brightest and at the same time the darkest he had ever seen, studied him as she responded sweetly, with a softness rich with hidden allusions: I came because of you, Nehemiah.

Nehemiah, as Sarah Izmosky recounts the event, stopped blushing and turned white. Sarah loved him, as did most of the girls in the class. She had no idea why Shlomzion had come to the party, and was in no position to grasp the calamity she had brought upon herself and her friends. Sarah brought Nehemiah a cup of lemonade unaware that at that moment she was filling her own cup with poison.

The courtship was brief yet romantic. Shlomzion did not believe in interim periods given to probing and introspection. She let Nehemiah woo her in an elegant manner with minor digressions, to disengage himself almost totally from close friends and admirers, to tell her strange amusing stories about the composition of matter, about remote birds that migrate to the Land of Israel, about amoebae, young settlers in the Galilee, the women of the Amazon, obscure forests, daring sea captains discovering islands in mysterious seas, his own bold and impossible love for her.

She heard the beat of war approaching. One day she proclaimed: Enough; either we marry or stop seeing each other.

He surrendered, they say, with unlimited liability, a life-and-death contract. When she brought him to Adonsky, who asked how much he was worth, Shlomzion responded with unprecedented valor: Nothing, but he'll learn!

To whom does he belong? Adonsky asked, as if he didn't know.

To Simha, she replied, deciding right then that if sallow Simha didn't die soon she would sever the bond between father and son.

The one who bought land for a bishlik and sold it for the same price?

Adonsky was alarmed. The lot on the corner of Allenby, the one my grandfather bought, the apple of his eye, sold by Simha for pennies, without profit, since war was approaching and he would no longer need a donkey?

Shlomzion said: He will learn. He is Simha's son by chance, not by nature. And one doesn't visit the sin of a father on his son! I met him, she said, with a show of frankness that did not escape her father's piercing eye, at the most awesome and most splendid moment of my life. I made him mine even before he knew me.

Adonsky was distraught. He had great plans for Shlomzion which were being shattered. He paced up and down, muttering: But how much is he worth? Why Simha, of all people? You know how I feel about that old man.... A poet and teacher ... Why not Abrams? He will become an important person. He is handsome. He knows how to do business. He's already worth a sizable sum. Why not the son of Asaf from Gedera, or Halfon's son? But Shlomzion was obstinate and Adonsky relented. The two were married after exactly three and a half years, several months after Adonsky bought the dunes directly southeast of Allenby and, to the amusement of the neighborhood, began referring to them as Rothschild Boulevard. Adonsky didn't laugh. He didn't know how to laugh. But even those who laughed did not laugh long. The wedding was an unforgettable event. Adonsky produced delicacies no one had ever seen before. Nehemiah's friends came because they were hungry. They had no faith in this marriage of Nehemiah and Shlomzion. It was a sin, a crime, to marry that cold and beautiful child; it was contrary to every tenet of the new pioneering faith to marry the daughter of a land speculator. But Adonsky celebrated lavishly. The war had just ended. There was still famine in the land. It was four years since anyone had tasted real food. At the wedding of Nehemiah and Shlomzion the guests feasted on chicken and potatoes, a variety of fish, caviar, champagne and excellent wines. Adonsky obtained these treasures from a young British officer in charge of providing supplies for officials of His Majesty's Government in Judea. The officer's account in Barclays Bank swelled overnight, offering striking evidence that war was not so intolerable.

From the day of their engagement until the wedding Nehemiah and Shlomzion remained an enigma to everyone. They kissed in dim rooms from which Shlomzion would emerge disheveled but proud. She loved Nehemiah as the spider loves its web. After the wedding they traveled to the United States, where he earned his doctorate while she complained about the American way of life. She said Americans were all stupid. When they went back home, there was tenderness between them, a quality no one could understand. But Nehemiah slept in the bed he laid out for himself. And she claims, to this day, that it was a royal one.

14

Aunt Shlomzion's yard is permeated with the scent of acacia and geranium—recalling a particular garden in Ramla with its splendid patio, Uncle Nehemiah engaged in conversation with a local scientist, educated in Heidelberg, on the subject of rare stamps and exotic birds. Now, standing before the tree planted by my uncle forty-five years back, I am dominated by an urge to tell the story of Shlomzion, the Great, to tell it in the idiom it dictates, gripping one's inner being with some sort of electromagnetic shock. There is a sudden wish to touch her, to love her, to be familial, indulgent, like Little Mother Shlomzion . . . to approach her through wrapping that is impermeable and irregular. I have, of late, been seeing plays, stylish and universal in scope, by a local writer who constructs evil figures, cardboard characters without guns but with a flow of wicked words, behaving badly to one another, tormenting each other, man-to-man villainy personified. I would like to write about love that transcends all this. I don't tend to thrive on caricature. Should one yield?

Shlomzion isn't cut of cardboard. She isn't a prima donna

tormenting Nehemiah and tormented with him. Shlomzion loves the Land of Israel. Her name suits her, a reference to Queen Shlomzion, that capricious tyrant whose name signified peace, who was full of vitality, totally destructive, tormented, tormenting, the intersection of a single moment with centuries, the genes of prodigies and charlatans, sudden tenderness and seething hate.

There is no such thing, the farmer said when they showed him a giraffe.

Mother Shlomzion tells how she finished her courses at the Teachers' Seminary. Nehemiah and Shlomzion have just returned from America. It is the year 1920. They lived in my grandmother's *pension* for a while. My grandmother began taking in roomers to support herself and her children after Simha died in the garret in 1917 while hiding from the Turks. The house was on Allenby Street. Is there a link between street and stress? Tryst and rest? Arrest and distress? Mother wore long dresses in those days—funny ones, at that. Aunt Shlomzion the Great had convinced Grandmother that Mother's legs were fat and ugly. Poor Mother didn't dare show her legs until it was too late. She studied diligently, helped her mother run the rooming house, lived an austere and modest life thinking how proud her father would have been to see her graduate from a teachers' seminary in the Land of Israel. Aunt Shlomzion in a silk dress and broad-brimmed Parisian hat, smelling of sweet perfume, knew nothing of pedagogy, but was an authority on legs.

Mother, she argued, was wasting her time; while she was young, it was her duty to make a vigorous effort to snare a husband. Later it would be too late.

It is a bright day in early summer. Mother is racing home, certificate in hand. The streets seem to be dancing. Little Mother Shlomzion is exuberant. On Allenby Street she passes a carriage loaded with young men who call to her. She waves. The world is aglow. The sun on one's skin washes away the remains of a dreary winter. Mr. Abrabanel is strolling down the street, sporting a striped suit and tie. He says: I see my little lady is laughing. She will, no doubt, bring great pleasure to her father (of blessed memory); I take this opportunity to invite her to a beautiful movie—Rudolph Valentino in a film filled with tears. The audience weeps, my dear, while Mr. Abrabanel's cashbox smiles.

The feel of the certificate is good. She is proud on behalf of her dead father. She had radical ideas about teaching reading in the primary grades. She showed the certificate to her mother with appropriate pride and characteristic modesty. Under her spectacles grandmother's eyes were brimming with tears. Mother said: I will be a good teacher, worthy of my father! It cannot be denied, her words had a pathetic ring. Still the moment was special, non-recurring, part of a great hour, a great period.

Years of study were not the convention. Food was scarce, as was money. When everyone returned to Tel Aviv after being evacuated to Kfar Saba, they were among those who didn't get a land grant. Grandfather died and they ate wild grass. It was then that Grandmother began to take in boarders, mainly teachers and poets. How much could they pay? Help was needed. There was laundry but no soap. Down on Allenby Street, in the dunes, Australian soldiers camped happily in tents. Through the window Abner and Little Shlomzion saw the tall Australians in their white undershirts, their faces red from the sun, eating sardines, cheese and butter. Grandmother used to make dresses from old sacks. We ate bulghur and eggplant, Mother recalls. One day an Australian soldier came and asked Grandmother for fresh bread at any price. He said: You have an oven—right? She answered, laughing: We have an oven but no flour. They began to negotiate, exchanging a series of implications, then a succession of doubts. He agreed to bring flour; Grandmother would bake bread every day and keep some of the leftover ingredients. When the soldier heard about the famine, he cried.

And so there was a temporary respite. Shlomzion the Great and Nehemiah were in America. Roads were being paved throughout the country at the time. Mother studied and worked, baked, cleaned, wore long dresses made from old flour sacks. On Saturdays she ran barefoot on the beach with young men who came from the north on horseback to see her. Adonsky took his gold supply and put up fifteen houses on Rothschild Boulevard. One of these, on the corner of Yavneh, was for himself—a fine and spacious structure topped by a little tower. Abner grew a mustache, went to Adonsky claiming he had been a licensed gardener in France and took on the landscaping. With his earnings he bought Grandmother an icebox. Adonsky was unaware that he was employing his son-in-law's brother. Had he known this, he never would have agreed. Simha's sons, he insisted, aren't worth even the artificial tear of a broken doll.

When they returned from America, before moving into their new house, Nehemiah and Shlomzion the Great lived in Grandmother's *pension* rather than in Adonsky's spacious house. Mother waited on Shlomzion, who appeared in a new silk dress every morning, wore Parisian hats and looked beautiful in the many mirrors she had brought with her from America.

Nehemiah went to work for Aaron Aronson in Zichron Yaakov and came home weekends, tired from the long ride on horseback. You see, Mother used to say to me, how much effort was involved in getting that certificate?

Aunt Shlomzion the Great was standing before the mirror. Mother came into the room. Grandmother will soon cry, then reach under her glasses to wipe the tears away. Shlomzion peered at the certificate, heard what Mother said and decreed: You will be a teacher from Esther's Fast to Purim, one whole day. Then she went out. Adonsky's carriage was waiting. They went off together to have lunch with the British general in Sharona. Mother taught in several schools for forty years. Now, when she comes to the private hospital in north Tel Aviv, Shlomzion the Great says: I, after all, know you married a young man, someone younger than me—so young, they say, that his hair is still black and he has the tender face of a boy. You must have bought him! Why don't you bring him to me? I won't steal him even if he falls in love with me.

She and her father dined with the British general. Later they ate ice cream there. My mother wept: from Esther's Fast until Purim! Forty years! How can it be explained? Is her father the clue? Maybe. They say very bizarre things about Adonsky. She is in him, he in her; she comes from him, she will go to him. She smiled when she told me about his funeral! Again I am in Shlomzion's garden, trying to understand Adonsky. Will an understanding of Adonsky make it possible to understand her?

Why is all this so important?

I don't know. Hard times. An apocalypse, maybe. It could be that all is over. The end of a dream. The price of Zionism may be its true motive, the swift conclusion of a people sacrificed on the altar of gold, oil and boredom. We will all die on color TV screens, viewed by billions of complacent citizens whose problems relate to galloping inflation and fishing on Sundays. Why now, of all times, between catastrophes? Why Shlomzion the Great? Why Adonsky?

All this is but a single tear lasting ninety years. Wherever you turn you will, in the end, arrive at rage and distress; also at a people's greatest splendor.

At the finish line the Garden of Eden seems so close! Reaching Adonsky is like reaching us all. Reaching another person implies love in the midst of massacre, faith that the miracle is in us.

15

Adonsky arrived in Jerusalem in the year 1871. No one knows where from. They say he was an army officer and fought in some war, then traveled to America, landing in Barbados, where he taught Hebrew to the boys and girls of a declining Jewish community, the oldest in the New World. He was seen in the streets of Constantinople, starving, and there are those who swear Adonsky was a leader of Jewish gangsters who terrorized the Odessa port. One old woman who lives in a crumbling hovel claims that Adonsky, a valiant fighter, was involved in a desperate battle in the port of Piraeus, or was it perhaps Fiume, and that his father was slain by a Cossack's axe. His own life, before arriving in Palestine, was enveloped in dense mist, which he made every effort to preserve, believing that the more opaque the past, the more promising the prospects for the present and the future. What brought him to the Land of Israel? He had no desire to be buried there, nor was he a pious man. He had contempt for the *halukkah* Jews living on charity in the four Holy Cities. Zionism didn't exist yet. He sometimes went to synagogue, even wore one of those broad hats, but no one in Jerusalem ever claimed

Adonsky was a faithful follower of the commandments.

The author of these pages is fond of family trees. I discovered that my great-grandfather on my mother's side arrived in the Land of Israel in 1860, preceding Adonsky by eleven years.

He came to die in Jerusalem, as was the custom then. He was sixty-two and, sensing that his end was near, wished to be buried on the Mount of Olives. In his dream, he reported, he was assigned to be a footstool for the Redeemer. That ancient forefather was ensconced on the Mount of Olives an entire year, rarely entering the city, even after the closing of the gates. He waited in a cave, eating carob and leaves, in eager anticipation. He prayed a great deal. People began to whisper that there was a holy man living on the mountain. They went to him seeking succor and salvation. Some rabbis opposed him, published charges and circulated them throughout the city. He knew nothing of this and the conflict was dissipated by his innocence. He is said to have been a very handsome man. He mixed medicines and wrote pamphlets containing striking calculations concerning the date of Redemption. But death, which he anticipated and on whose behalf he had abandoned a wife and children in Odessa, seemed to tarry.

After a year he went down to Jerusalem and delivered several learned discourses. They say that even those rabbis who had opposed him earlier attended his words in awe and astonishment. He bought a burial plot. After going down into the city and realizing that Death was detained somewhere, he sold the plot at a profit. Not that he sought profit; but, having put the plot on the market, he was offered a sum twice what he had paid a year earlier.

These facts reached Adonsky's ears. Adonsky knew very few things, but what he did know he knew well. He knew my great-grandfather long before his own daughter's birth, long before she stood on the Jaffa shore feeling the five shells streak through her exquisite hair and decided, thereupon, to bind her lot with that of Nehemiah, descendant of that old man from the Mount of Olives.

How did Adonsky know?

Little Mother Shlomzion maintains that everything is chance, whereas I maintain that all things are connected by links the mind doesn't fathom. Adonsky knew my great-grandfather but didn't understand him. He grasped the principle, seemingly simple, that the price of a burial plot on the Mount of Olives doubles in a year. This is a rule with land, since it is no longer being produced.

When the old man lived in town, he continued to be aware that his end was approaching. Every week, on Thursdays, the day on which he predicted he would die, he used to go up to the Mount of Olives and await the Redeemer in throes of agony over his expected end. His skin was already shriveled. People nodded sympathetically, exclaiming: He came to die, but he lives on!

He bought himself another burial plot, which he sold at a profit. Adonsky knew this, too. My great-grandfather lived on this profit, never accepting charity, and died at the age of eighty-eight, on the seventh of Adar, which is the day of Moses' death, having sustained himself until the end. That morning he had gone up to the Mount of Olives and, taking leave of the old widow who used to clean his house, he said: I will not return; we shall see each other again on the wings of the Messiah.

He did not return.

He crept into his grave to wait, and died there.

He died with a smile frozen on his face.

His grave was desecrated by the Jordanians.

Two of his offspring destroyed Assam Kassani's grave about fifteen years ago so the Hilton Hotel could be built in its place.

Adonsky already knew then that life in this country is difficult and complex, that even lands destined for life are no more than the burial ground of the future. When he arrived in Jerusalem, he went directly to the Mount of Olives, measured off some plots, contacted the various burial societies that hold the keys to the gates of paradise and began selling burial plots to Jews from Russia and Poland. He dispatched letters and certificates of sale, as well as hundreds of little bags of earth from the Holy Land for the benefit of those whose lot it was to die in the lands of dispersion, also holy Jordan water in bottles to cure heart disease, rheumatism and countless other ailments. He once struck an Arab who told him to put on his hat, which was required of Jews. The following day Adonsky arranged asylum for himself and triple citizenship (Austrian, British, Russian). Adonsky knew that the Mount of Olives was closer (physically) to the footfalls of Redemption than any other mountain in the world. He also knew that in the amphitheatre of Redemption there were seats that were more desirable, as well as less desirable ones. For instance, anyone buried facing the Temple Mount would get a first glimpse of the Messiah and be restored to the world of the living before the others. Furthermore, space on the Mount of Olives was becoming scarce, while the number of deceased wishing to be buried in the Holy Land was growing at a steady pace. Indeed, Adonsky's eloquent letters did not fail to elicit a response. The customers increased rapidly, though the land supply did not increase in a similar proportion. The plots became smaller and Adonsky built himself a fine and spacious house in Jerusalem.

He believed only in gold currency and exchanged all his other monies, even if it involved a slight loss. In this way he maintained a single index that applied to all his enterprises. His dead arrived in the Land of Israel very old and alone, to be buried on the Mount of Olives in plots that grew smaller and smaller. Still, they were pleased with their fate. The dead don't see where they are buried and there were no families present. So everyone was satisfied: Adonsky; the burial societies, whose share in the profit was increasing; the rabbis and cantors; even the relatives, who didn't have to finance funerals and received from Adonsky an announcement signed by two rabbis certifying that their flesh and blood was indeed buried on the Mount of Olives and at the moment when the dead are revived would be companions to angels and God, that He who provides peace in His heaven would provide peace for us and the entire house of Israel. Amen.

In private conversation with two Jerusalem rabbis Adonsky argued that the dimensions of a dead man were not the same as his dimensions when alive; that man, born tiny, grows to full size, and that when he dies he is reduced to the size of an embryo. The graves, therefore, must be large enough to accommodate a newborn baby. That, in any case, is God's scheme, he said. Why should a body be placed in a grave that measures a meter and a half if in only two months the body will shrink to ten by eighty centimeters? All those bones waiting to rise again have the volume of a newborn.

They didn't accept his argument. But when he reduced the dimensions of the plots they raised no objections.

In this manner Adonsky amassed a fortune that was considerable, though not excessive.

Not yet.

When his position was secure, Adonsky took Miriam, Rabbi Ben-Amram's daughter, as his wife. Miriam was a slim, fair-haired girl, with an expression of dismay that had registered on her face once and remained imprinted on it always. Ben-Amram was an emissary of the Hebron community who went forth with the well-known Shneur-Zalman, son of Menahem-Mendel, to Baghdad and Egypt. Then he spent many years traveling through the lands of North Africa, returned to Hebron, took a wife, penned several books, one of which had already been written by a scholar from the Beth-El Yeshiva in Jerusalem. He brought a large sum of money and letters from distinguished rabbis, as well as considerable secrets relating to the Sambatyon River and the ten lost tribes. After Miriam and her two brothers were born, he went on another mission to Egypt, then to Yemen, and, after riding many long months, to Basra. From there he sailed to India. In Calcutta he addressed the community and obtained a letter from a Hebrew-speaking rabbi who was the chief of a daring desert tribe, a conquerer of many lands. He went on to Persia, and, finally, returned to Hebron.

During the cholera epidemic in 1860, he invoked important incantations and charms and was generally helpful in the task of sustaining the sick and burying the dead. He was tall and bright-eyed, with a fierce quality, impelled by violent fury. When Miriam was fifteen, he embarked on a new voyage, this time to Europe, following in the footsteps of Hayim Yosef David Azulai. He visited cities in Germany and Italy, reaching as far as Amsterdam, from whence he dispatched a large sum of money, as well as letters and an excellent composition on the subject of martyrdom. Placing these in the hands of another emissary from the Land of Israel, who chanced to cross his path, he himself set forth for Barbados where he visited the grave of Rabbi Karigal, from Hebron, who had died there a hundred years earlier. Ben-Amram followed his footsteps to Providence, Rhode Island, and delivered an interesting discourse there on the Third Temple, in the very synagogue in which Karigal had preached. When he returned to Hebron, bringing a large sum of money, young men danced in the streets, Hassidic dances pure and devout. He wrote a book, working feverishly and with quiet wrath. He locked himself in his room, dismissing his entire family from his presence until it was finished. Then he placed the book in a sealed chest and disappeared with it into the depths of the Machpelah Cave, the cave of the patriarchs.

The Muslims were outraged; the Jews were outraged. They would have come to blows but for the Turkish governor and his police force, who surrounded the cave, searched it and, failing to find the culprit, convinced both Jews and Muslims that the cave was empty.

But he was actually inside. Two days and two nights he sat weeping over the grave of our father Abraham.

Then Ben-Amram went to Jerusalem, obtained letters from prominent rabbis addressed to the Jewish community at the Sambatyon River and to the leaders of the ten tribes, as well as to the king of Hibernia, and set forth for Europe. From there he moved on to Basra, collecting the largest sum ever, and vanished. In his last letter he wrote: To my brothers dwelling in the Vale of Tears. I have discovered marvelous things, and I am embarking on a journey. I have abundant funds, countless coins as well as astonishing writings [letters?] concerning our brother Rav Karigal, the ten lost tribes, renowned rabbis and valiant Jewish soldiers. My affection forever to my daughter Miriam and my wife, also to my two sons. Another letter, more detailed, will be sent to you through a channel I myself was afraid to follow. From me, Ben-Amram, your slave and emissary from Hebron, a city that bewails its sons in the Vale of Stupefaction beside the burial place of our forefathers, may their memory be blessed.

He never returned. They waited in vain.

Hebron was astir over the loss of the money for many days.

Other emissaries claimed that they saw Ben-Amram in Damascus.

Still others swore that he had appeared before them in a forest near Cologne, Germany. According to one theory, he had converted and others maintained that he was serving as a rabbi in some South African city flowing with gold and diamonds.

Miriam and her mother remained alone. Her two brothers went to live in Safed. Their small house was surrounded by bitter people who never forgot throughout that turbulent period of the wars of Ibrahim Pasha, the drought and famine. Miriam awaited her father's return. Her sharp tongue and her close relationship to her father alienated the young men, though there was not a woman in Hebron or Jerusalem more beautiful and delicate than she was. Her beauty was alarming. Young men would catch sight of her sitting at the window and fall to the ground in a faint. One such young man was watching her from his window in Hebron when two small clouds appeared suddenly, hiding the light of day from him forever after. Others suffered temporary impairment. They feared her, yet found themselves circling her house, mumbling, often shamefully aroused. The mother would chase them, cursing, to which they would retort: Where is Ben-Amram? He has abandoned you, old woman!

Adonsky heard about Miriam, Ben-Amram's daughter, from a Jew who came to buy a burial plot for his father in Lublin. Adonsky sent messengers to Miriam who returned with no response. Adonsky's love was all the more intense, his passions stirred, when the messengers returned with Miriam's hostile glare fixed on their faces, clinging to them obstinately. Deep inside of him something was touched. Hate touched hate, anger matched anger. And so he found himself desperately in love with a woman he had never seen. He felt the two furies, his and Miriam's, entwined together, in a single wreath.

One winter day Adonsky bridled his horse, which he had bought from a bandit in Trans-Jordan and fitted with a handsome saddle from Damascus. He set off for Hebron. It was a cold journey. Adonsky rode through clouds, his spirits high, his breath frosty. Tightly wrapped against the cold, people were slinking through the narrow streets. The mountains glistened for a moment in the fierce sunlight only to be erased a few seconds later by dense fog. It was the month of Adar. There was snow in the air, though it had not begun to fall. The air was sticky and sharp. Adonsky loved riding into the lashing wind: he loved the creviced mountain. The horse was foaming. Adonsky sang aloud to himself. He had never sung before and his own voice was strange to him, as if someone else were singing through him.

He arrived in Hebron shortly before the snow began falling. While searching for Miriam's house, he was accosted by a group of young men dressed like ravens who mocked and jeered at him, declaring: Here comes the grave-dealer to call on the daughter of the fence-smasher, who awaits him eagle-eyed, wielding a certificate concerning the ten lost tribes and a whip. One young man appeared to be especially incensed. His eyes brimming with enmity and indignation, he shouted: Go to that woman and you'll return a dog!

Adonsky dismounted and approached the young man, speaking calmly: I have an excellent plot in the Mount of Olives as yet unoccupied. One more word and you will see both Messiahs, David's son as well as Joseph's, wrapped in one, though it is many good years too soon, and I fear that neither dry bones nor even broken ones will remain of you to be restored to life. Then he raised his voice and shrieked: *Etlala!*

Through streets filled with the odor of charred meat and pungent herbs, violent winds, clouds heavy with snow, the young men fled for their lives. Had he known how Adonsky would have laughed, for deep within him something monumental was laughing.

By the time the snowflakes began to fall all of Hebron was informed that Adonsky had arrived and spoken harshly to Rabbi Azulai's son.

Azulai left his house, his face flushed, to wait for Adonsky in the razor-sharp wind. When Adonsky approached and greeted him, Azulai said: Get down from the animal, sir, and declare yourself. Otherwise, you shall be cursed, molester of schoolchildren.

Adonsky, who was quick to recognize power, dismounted and said: I hit no one. I was provoked and responded. The people of Israel are responsible for one another.

The Rabbi waited, in angry silence.

Then Adonsky took a sheet of paper from his pocket which he flashed under the Rabbi's eyes, whispering some words in his ear. A woman peering out of a window above swears he whispered the following: My name is Adonsky; my father was Ben-Klonymos, author of *Maadanei Yisrael*, [*Delectations of Israel*], by Ben-Amram; you will surely have the sense to hear my story, the wisdom to comprehend it and the kindness to welcome a Jew arriving from the Holy City of Jerusalem on a snowy night through a storm that will rage three days and three nights.

The snowflakes were thicker now. The Rabbi's ear was attentive as he scrutinized the tall man standing beside his festively arrayed horse, and the rage began to subside.

Adonsky continued to speak (so the woman reported): I know the renowned Ben-Amram; I know his origins. I am the only man in the world who truly knows what happened to him. Also, I know the whereabouts of the money he was to bring to Hebron. . . .

And the amount.

And how to obtain it.

I know things that the wise rabbi from Hebron, whoever he may be, has been seeking for many years in books that are ancient but incorrect, facts about the ten tribes, the Sambatyon River and incredible calculations about the year of Redemption. I know these things from Ben-Amram, who acquired them from someone who studied with the Holy ARI. I even know it was the wise rabbi himself who sent Ben-Amram on his final mission. And only I know what transpired between them: what the rabbi said to Ben-Amram, what Ben-Amram said to the rabbi (whoever that rabbi may be). I know why that clever rabbi withholds from his holy community the fact that Ben-Amram did, indeed, stay in the Machpelah Cave and hear our father Abraham speak to him, that he returned from there his body unblemished. I have the power to assist this same wise rabbi in spiritual matters as well as those with material elements and, regardless of climate or elements, to be helpful in an exchange that does not, of course, involve any special effort on the part of a wise rabbi who understands one thing from another, whose cleverness requires no further allusions.

The people rushing home at the sight of the great snowstorm caught a glimpse of Azulai's glowing anxious face. He was seen bending low, despite the heavy snow and powerful wind, whispering: May you be blessed! He lifted his eyes and proclaimed: Your home is mine, Rabbi Adonsky. The two of them went in immediately. The horse was led to the stable, and Adonsky spent three days and three nights in Azulai's house. Many stories were related in Hebron about these three days. Shlomzion neither confirms nor denies them. Clearly, these tales were all meant for Miriam's ears. And every word that was said did indeed reach her. Adonsky once told his Arab that his wife, Miriam, really was very beautiful, that he never loved her as he did before they actually met. He told the Arab of his love for Miriam during those three wondrous days in snowy Hebron, a town removed from the world, engaged in heating its houses and viewing the heavy skies as if the world were at an end—a love that was the most wondrous event of his life.

They say sparks were seen flying through the room on that first night. The conversation between Rabbi Azulai and Adonsky was so animated and excited that every few minutes the two of them would get up and join in a long embrace. Even the windows blazed, a neighbor woman reports, and there are others supporting her description, as though a fierce sun had fallen into the house. There were those who sat three nights observing Azulai's windows. The privileged class, whose houses looked out on Azulai's, sold window space like in synagogues.

They say that on the second night Azulai's son was brought in to beg Adonsky's forgiveness, that he fell on his knees five times beseeching pardon. It was two weeks before he returned to his place in school, and it was noted that something in his eyes had grown dim and died. They say the boy was silent for five years, not saying a word. Even during the cholera epidemic, when people chattered as if possessed, seeing visions, prophesying in the streets, attempting to arrest the plague with incantations and charms, he didn't utter a word, only continued mumbling his prayers. After three days and three nights Rabbi Azulai went out for morning prayers. It was no longer snowing. The city was draped in white; the sun gave off blinding light. He was transformed. Upon entering the synagogue, he embraced Adonsky and began praying in a majestic voice that rent heaven and earth. His eyes sparkled.

Adonsky had met Ben-Amram on the Mount of Olives two years earlier. He didn't know then that Ben-Amram had a daughter and that this daughter would one day be his wife and mother of his beloved child Shlomzion. He was standing beside a burial plot he had sold to a highly pedigreed family of rabbis from Hungary. The sun had just begun to set and the Mosque of Omar glowed with golden light that startled his extinguished eyes. Facing the golden splendor of the dome that seemed to rise above the darkening abyss, he felt himself an ember in the vast fire, contracting, then reduced to nothing. Suddenly there was someone at his side. He hadn't noticed when the Hungarian slipped away and another man appeared. The man said: I am Ben-Amram, bereft of myself. Adonsky considered these words worth investigating. It was a chilly summer night and the two men sat down to talk. Adonsky offered Ben-Amram wine; Ben-Amram offered roasted watermelon seeds. Ben-Amram told Adonsky how Rabbi Azulai of Hebron had sent him to find traces of the ten tribes and to bring support for his theory, full of suspense and peril, that the Messiah son-of-David would precede the Messiah son-of-Joseph. He had written letters to rabbis whose names were odd and baffling, to places no one had heard of, seeking answers to important questions that filled one with terror. Ben-Amram told Adonsky how he had once been standing at a river in a distant land, a river that was bright and desolate, that he suddenly saw a huge fish advancing toward him and watched the fish perform amazing feats, transforming the still brilliance of the water, then changing its own form, becoming something else. He knew then; he suddenly knew that his name was no longer what it had been, that he was totally different from the man who had arrived at the water a short time earlier. He had been looking for himself ever since, sometimes even assuming the look of his own self, he said. He forgot he had a family in Hebron. He locked all the windows. Just a few days ago, traveling from Sidon to Damascus, he regained his former consciousness and a fire sprung from his eyes, leading him to think that locking himself in and opening himself up anew had some noble significance. He thought, so he told Adonsky, that Providence may have destined him to seek answers to questions no one had asked. Today, he muttered sadly, he is inclined to suspect that Rabbi Azulai was exploiting him for undefined purposes, not altogether innocent ones; that Azulai was, in fact, aware that he had been in the Machpelah Cave and heard Abraham speak, yet neither said nor suggested this to the people of the city. Illuminated by a mysterious light, Ben-Amram continued to tell about the Sambatyon River, to relate answers he had found without knowing what questions they referred to. He spoke of Jewish girls carrying swords and shields, going out to do battle at their husbands' sides and vanquishing fierce desert bandits. He told of meeting an aged man who revealed secrets of Redemption transmitted by a student of the Holy ARI. Also, that the years 5720–5736 would be an era of struggle and destruction; that in the year 5736 mighty armies from the north and south would attack God's people and that in that year, 5736, while the earth caused the Holy City to tremble, the accursed mosque would sink and be replaced by a mountain elevated above the hills and containing remnants of the Temple and its ancient menorah. Hailstones would fall from heaven— Then would our righteous Messiah appear to rescue our surviving remnant and a new era would dawn unmarked by time, unmarred by good and evil, filled with love of God, perfection, eternal progress toward the binding of fragments. . . . He presented evidence for all this from the Book of Daniel. Rabbi Azulai, he said, had sought some of these things from him; he had found others for himself and there were still others about which he would disclose nothing further. He had come to Jerusalem, so he said, to find a burial plot, for it was his intention to return someday and find rest here and a legacy in his other name, thus outsmarting the evil spirits that conspired to burn him and consume his spirit. He would be buried alongside his family unbeknownst to them. Adonsky knew that Ben-Amram was not deranged.

Adonsky understood what had befallen him.

Ben-Amram described visions he had seen, the searing words perched on the edge of his tongue, which he was afraid to utter. He gave Adonsky a huge sum of money and said: I collected these funds while traveling as an emissary. I myself never touched them. I never betrayed the trust. As soon as my person changed, I changed my ethic as well. But I never touched the money. It is all here, dedicated to the Holy City of Hebron and its blessed community. I arrived from myself to myself for a single moment. Now I mean to deliver myself and leave this place. I have no stake in Ben-Amram and it is no virtue to be who I was. God asked that I become someone else, and, like Avram who became Abraham, I shall become a man whose name even you will not know.

Adonsky remembered everything. This is not the place to review all the secrets. The story of the secrets is not relevant to Shlomzion's story, apart from the phrase "from himself to himself," which she transformed into "I conceived in and of myself." She is now lying in the hospital in north Tel Aviv, despising the world through veils of glittering beauty, waiting for infinite revenge that was, perhaps, born in that river as it engulfed her grandfather and made him into someone else. It is only right to mention the fact that what Adonsky told Rabbi Azulai was shocking and full of secrets and answers; that Miriam's mother was no longer considered an abandoned wife, nor was Ben-Amram regarded as a charlatan. He was dead, Adonsky reported, having died the following day, and was buried on the Mount of Olives under his assumed name. Both his name and his will were in Adonsky's pocket. He bequeathed his burial plot to whosoever would inform the people of Israel of the Messiah's approach. His other name was known only to Adonsky and Rabbi Azulai, to them alone.

Rabbi Azulai said: Ben-Amram saw our father Abraham. He strove with death and damnation, struggled with angels, beheld the searing fire of the Name and was burned by it, burned so that we might know. We will not reveal his identity. We will not disclose his secret. May his soul be bound in the bond of life.

In the synagogue he said: I have heard many things about Ben-Amram. He is dead. He was holy. He was a messenger but we failed to recognize him; God's messenger, not ours. Miriam may well be proud of her father, and her brothers have every right to return to Hebron. There is no pride greater than pride in a father who sets forth to burn fire, burns it and is burned.

Rabbi Azulai wrote one hundred books which made him known throughout the world.

Not one of these books is remembered.

And, as for Adonsky, he struck a winning bargain. Miriam was rescued from loneliness and hostility. Even the most hardened and bitter women kissed her. Her mother cried relentlessly for a week and died at the end of that happy period. Her heart could bear no more. Miriam fell in love with Adonsky before they met. She was aroused by the words, the intensity, the intimacy with her father, the tunes Adonsky transmitted through the walls of Hebron's houses, buried in snow that was level with windows and doors, following the most severe storm in fifty years, at least.

16

In the afternoon I was in the hospital again with Shlomzion, trying to understand this beautiful woman who, at seventy-six, was waiting eagerly for the young doctor with stylishly gray hair to arrive. I was trying to probe the Hebron disaster of almost a century ago. She refuses to answer questions. For her, Hebron is a sealed chapter. Even after the Six-Day War she didn't go to Hebron. Her love of the land is abstract. She visited Haifa only once. When she went to Europe with Adonsky, they embarked from the Haifa port. She was never on the Carmel or in the Emek. When Nehemiah traveled to other parts of the country, she stayed home and sighed. She loved being saturated with cool gray vitality at the peak of a heat wave. She was not acquainted with the anguished shrieking out-of-doors. She was in Jerusalem only twice in her adult life. She lived in her own Land of Israel, secret and very abstract. Which may be how she knew hate. Saints, generals and madmen are well versed in abstract hatred, possessing a hidden and invisible capacity to understand processes. Shlomzion never did touch life with her hands, living in unending gentility. But she knew several things she never articulated. She loved in herself, and perhaps even more so in her father and her grandfather, the sense of chained flight, the lunaticlike dance under the stars, that ancient dance of great poets who withhold their poems rather than let them be heard, for each potential listener is an actual enemy. Adonsky and Ben-Amram set out to seek a world they themselves invented. Their passions were excessive and they lived among people who devised moral standards and binding systems that did not fit them. Adonsky and Ben-Amram touched devils, touched hell and returned, undiminished, blazing with a fire others didn't see.

Adonsky spent those three nights in Hebron talking. Not everything that was said is known. People swear the Rabbi's house was enveloped in fog all through the night, that only a window was visible. The snow, they said, melted on the window as soon as it fell. I read Ben-Amram's buried book. I traced his origins. One day I will write these things in a book. Ben-Amram followed the track of Karigal, a Hebronite who went to America two hundred and fifty years ago and preached the construction of a Third Temple in Providence, Rhode Island. I found a rare copy of Ben-Amram's book, tattered and yellow with age. But the year is now 1974. In two years it will be 5736 (since the creation of the world). Redemption is near. The earth will burst asunder. Stones will be catapulted from the sky. I said to Little Mother Shlomzion: Listen here, Ben-Amram foresaw the War of Independence. He said it would occur in 5709. He missed by one year; it was actually 5708. He described the Six-Day War from clues in the Book of Daniel and calculations based on Ezekiel. He relates an account by the great ARI of the Yom Kippur War (which he thought would break out on Sukkot) hundreds of years before it occurred. Why not believe in Redemption preceded by destruction? The enemy comes from north and south, armed with weapons from the icy lands. Metal birds will crowd the sky and stones as large as the Temple will be hurled at them. The hour of judgment will bring both solace and destruction. Rivers of blood will give way to rivers of appeasement and charity. Stars will descend from the sky; people from other worlds will return to us; the dead will rise up; our people, Israel, will become a powerful nation of many million. One third of those living in Zion (Ben-Amram wrote this at a time when there were a few thousand Jews inhabiting the four Holy Cities) will be destroyed; two million will survive. After the dead revive, they will reproduce and multiply two hundred and fifty times. Redemption will descend on us like a great sigh and will be filled with contentment steeped in longing. Shlomzion is an advance reading of her father's book. She is, perhaps, an allusion to Jewish duality; we endure but remain somewhere beyond history. Or is she merely an old woman who will never die? I will leave the books and secrets for brighter days, I told Little Mother Shlomzion. There is so much sadness and yearning now; why add pain to discomfort?

Miriam of Hebron was married to Adonsky. Her mother was buried, free of charge, in a plot adjacent to her husband's. Old Nahumi is unwilling to speculate about Miriam's love for Adonsky. But he knows that Adonsky and Miriam loved each other madly, with fierce passion, during the three days and nights preceding their meeting. Miriam was a handsome woman. After leaving Hebron she never returned to her birthplace. She never wanted to go to Hebron. She didn't visit her mother's grave. After moving to Jaffa with Adonsky she neglected the commandments she had been trained to observe since childhood. Adonsky, she told Dr. Hissin once, is a cloth sewed from my father's charred body. She amended her statement: a shroud, perhaps a prayer shawl.

Adonsky and his wife arrived in Jaffa in the late eighteen-seventies. It was a fine spring day. Citrus trees filled the air with a sweet pungent scent. In the north the sand stretched to the edge of the earth. Very few Jews lived in Jaffa at the time. The sea licked the steps of the houses lining the port. No one understood what Adonsky was up to in Jaffa, why he would leave his flourishing enterprises—trading in graves, for example—to come to a small town with no future. They were not aware that Adonsky was spinning a marvelous yarn from pet devils, avenging two thousand years of humiliation. Ben-Amram, who was dead, was his only friend at the time. He spoke to him in dreams. Adonsky considered himself responsible for the inheritance bequeathed by Ben-Amram.

Adonsky went down to Jaffa expecting other Jews. He knew they would come. According to Ben-Amram's calculations, the century of destruction and Redemption would begin in 1876 C.E. lasting until 5735—one hundred years. During this interval, monumental changes would occur. Jews would come and a Jewish state would be established; but there would also be widespread destruction and terrible catastrophes, unlike anything known. Blood would be spilled, but the people of Israel would try to repair the havoc. Hidden lights with brilliant beams piercing the shells encasing them would reverse the order in heaven. God would go to war, be struck down and, in the end, prevail. Who is like you among the gods, O Lord? . . . God's enemies will be scattered in every direction. . . . Adonsky waited for these events to unfold. It is odd to think of Adonsky, the land speculator, as first to be redeemed.

Before the Zionists arrived in the Land of Israel, Adonsky was there waiting with his unsung anthems, waving flags that had neither shape nor distinction, wishing to be redeemed, to bring himself out of Egypt, enacting the Exodus every year, redeeming and being redeemed. Land is the key. It must be possessed, though it responds to its lovers and to those who possess it with rage and enmity. Adonsky knew the Turkish Empire was crumbling. He knew that its system of land administration would be a stimulus to settlement, grasping this before anyone, as soon as the first wave of new believers arrived—rejecting the faith in Messiahs, seeking some new hymns, melancholy and hopeful in the charmed land coveted by their forefathers. But, in the meanwhile, Turks occupied the port. Famine and sickness were all around. Full boats sailed away from the shore as growing numbers of people were overcome with despair. Adonsky, whose prophetic vision was linked to the gold exchange and to concern for his non-liquid assets, was in mourning. A great man, they said, cursing him in Yiddish, Russian and broken modern Hebrew.

So Adonsky went down to Jaffa.

He was prepared for the future, prepared for Zionism packaged in his own measured, pragmatic terms. He himself was not a Zionist. He never voted in a Congress, didn't meddle in politics, join societies or sing stirring songs into the night.

He used to leave home in the morning, early. The markets were still empty; the butchers were hanging inverted lamb carcasses on heavy pegs. There were mounds of tomatoes and greens, the sound of barbers sharpening their implements, the sea at times turbulent, at times quiet—the roar of a marketplace without people, as yet without people. It was an hour suited for infinite affection. Adonsky on his horse, accompanied by his Arab, sets off to survey land. Adonsky explains to Herr Wolff, the German spy, his love for the shrewdness and exhilarating corruption of the Turks. Everything has its price, a price that changes regularly. Every man has a set figure that shifts within securely defined limits. People can be bought by consulates and granted new citizenship. This is how the Turkish Empire is being dismembered. Ralbag, from Hebron, is now Rabinowitz.

I read important messages in Shlomzion's eyes: Zionism is Adonsky's invention, an invention he himself did not adopt.

For a love of the Land of Israel belongs to Adonsky.

There is no street named for him in the entire country, though there is no city that doesn't owe its existence and development to Adonsky.

He is the pole; they are but humble flags, Shlomzion said.

The matter of Pobedonostsev may be relevant here. He was an adviser to Czar Alexander III, who taught him a very important principle: oppress Jews vigorously; never relent, persist until a third of them perish, a third convert and a third leave Russia.

These words, particularly those at the end of the formulation, were the basis of Adonsky's thinking. He even declared at the meeting of Tel Aviv founders (after refusing to live in the new neighborhood developing around the lot where Yemenites originally built their houses, a neighborhood that was becoming a city circling Yemenite vineyards long since abandoned to sorrow) that the name Tel Aviv was especially suitable because of its Oriental Arab ring. The local people, he suggested (others nodded in agreement), will find the name easy to pronounce.

Adonsky sat in Jaffa (Yafo) and said: The root of Jaffa is *yofi*, beauty in Hebrew, and is also related to the Greek. He invoked an appropriate play on words from Job, which he described as an optimistic book. The letters of *yofi* can be reversed, suggesting a promise for the future, a fortress on the sea open to all, built on a pyramid of skulls by Napoleon, faltering and fleeing from devastating blows. On this rock in the sea, opposite the window, Andromeda was sacrificed to the sea god. In Jerusalem they quibble endlessly over the laws of the Seventh (Sabbatical) year and how they apply to the new settlement. The position of Jaffa is thereby consolidated. There are lands to be bought here. A great new settlement will develop. Jaffa will be a center, the port of the future for the flying catapults of Redemption.

In the year 1892 the railroad from Jaffa to Jerusalem was dedicated. The train station was built near Neveh Shalom.

Here, through Adonsky's initiative (perhaps not through his initiative alone) various enterprises were set up dealing in munitions, provisions, export-import and, later on, agricultural equipment.

Jerusalem will remain preoccupied with the recesses of the past, while here on the sands we will construct a nation from the land. A new nation is to be created from an old-new land. Jaffa, rich in fabrics, fragrances, fresh fish roasted on coals, cool lemon slivers—Jaffa is the pearl of the world, he proclaimed.

17

Adonsky's great day dawned when the first Zionists arrived in the Land of Israel. Adonsky was among the few individuals in Jaffa who were not stunned by rumors of Jews planning to come and work the land, to be farmers, to build houses. He was expecting them.

He knew it was not merely a fleeting prank but a reversal of history, one he envisioned long ago. One might say that in those burial plots on the Mount of Olives he anticipated a Jewish state. Just as Herzl was gripped by his vision while gazing over a bridge in Basel, Adonsky's vision unfolded midst the graves of obstinate individuals whose wish it was to die in the Holy Land. He knew with clarity devoid of dismay or malice, yet without excessive affection, that a day was nigh dedicated to those wishing to live in the primal melancholy of God's domesticated tear, to cultivate the harsh soil of that bleak rocky mass.

Rabbi Yekutiel, an emissary from Safed, was incredulous, recounting impressions of young Jews encountered in Constantinople. They look, he said, like the Americans in the American colony near Jaffa (where German Templars live now), and speak of Jewish settlement and national revival, using Hebrew as a spoken tongue. Adonsky shocked several of Jaffa's most erudite citizens by nodding and declaring that he had been expecting them for some time now. Drinking coffee from small cups and smoking narghiles with the Turkish governor, men laughed at the new Jews and their schemes.

Adonsky did not laugh.

He didn't laugh for two reasons. Because he had faith; also because his muscles were not equipped for laughter. Adonsky's mouth was somewhat twisted. He tried laughing once. Everyone was alarmed, concluding that his Arab was dead and he was in mourning, since it was known that only two things could cause him distress: the death of his daughter Shlomzion or the death of his Arab. Shlomzion was at his side, so there was no cause for concern on her account. They didn't realize he was trying to smile. He always worried about the welfare of his Arab, who could name all the flowers and plants, also inform him who was selling and when. (Assam Kassani arrived in Jaffa some years later.)

This Arab knew the quality of land. He knew all about that type of malaria-bearing mosquito that tends to abandon an area for a period of weeks only to return and infest it. He knew the environment, the perils of land certificates. He was an ideal guide for Adonsky in his early ventures. Later on, when Adonsky no longer needed instruction or guidance, the Arab was like an artificial limb.

The early Zionist settlers were received by Adonsky with chilly enthusiasm. They interested him because of their business potential. Their enthralling visions had a quality that was too desperate and murky to stir his heart. They were obstinate about a faith that struck him as amorphous. He refused to share their exhilarating vision of settlement, much as he loved this land which responded to him, to his forced possession, with astonishing vitality. He could not comprehend the hearts of tea merchants and peddlers suddenly determined to farm like the Arabs.

But, let it be said in his favor, he was undisturbed by this lack of comprehension. Adonsky relished the scent of gold. Aunt Shlomzion the Great grew up in a household where a gold coin was grounds for festivity, where coins were studied and celebrated. Shlomzion learned to weave them into sonnets that were restrained yet passionate, to help pass the heat or chill of night in her room in the big house in Jaffa.

Mornings Adonsky would go to the market and from there set off on horseback in the company of his Arab, who was known to bite the earth with his teeth, so profound was his need to please, to be loved, to see sparks leaping in Adonsky's eyes. He would decree: This is good land! He knew what was good for wheat, what was suited for citrus. He identified smells and vegetation and told tales that conveyed the wisdom of generations. Adonsky learned secrets from him that only a skilled merchant such as he could exploit.

Miriam, Shlomzion's mother, guarded her beauty as if it were an ornament. She brought with her an odd sort of rigor, domesticated savagery, muted rage that moaned like a wounded dog. After the three-day period when her love for Adonsky flourished though she had never seen him, she receded into her own shadow, on the road to the oblivion she craved. She despised Adonsky so for causing her to fall in love with him for three superfluous days, sublime days filled with vague and fraudulent radiance, that she was ready to die if this would inconvenience him.

Miriam's frailness was the talk of Jaffa. At first she used to go to the rabbis for remedies and special formulas. They invoked spirits of singular personalities on her behalf, and from time to time Adonsky's tightly clenched hand favored them with gifts, though more often he cursed and chastised them.

Miriam receded into her own shadow with a proud aristocratic smile. She learned to cherish rare beauty, elusive, tamed, enclosed in a box. For this is how Adonsky saw her. She cultivated an affinity, mysterious and discriminating, for the precious stones she had begun to collect avidly. Hers was a highly refined sensibility. Even from a distance she could distinguish the gleam of an emerald or a sapphire. She bought and sold gems without the knowledge of her husband, who was busy chewing the earth, selling and expanding the borders of his empire like Ahab, the ancient King, his idol and redeemer.

Miriam, the bitter one, had a red leather suitcase filled with precious jewels worth a considerable fortune. She assumed Adonsky was aware of its existence.

Whenever Adonsky refused to pay the rabbis or doctors for formulas or medicines, Miriam would give them a jewel. They would sell these jewels to Adonsky at a slightly inflated price and he, when in Beirut buying land, would sell them at an even more inflated price to Englishmen who come to the east to be close to God, to retrieve dead or lost martyrs, to discover roots in the desert or to photograph the tormented route of Jesus.

So the entire transaction was to everyone's advantage and no one was any the worse for it.

And Shlomzion learned things that no school for girls or even a first Hebrew Gymnasia in two thousand years was equipped to impart.

Adonsky had no regrets even when he discovered that he had just paid five francs for a jewel his wife had sold for three. He didn't complain. He made up the difference, not caring who was the first to profit.

Shlomzion loved Adonsky. She never mentions Miriam. She remembers him welcoming English, German and American tourists arriving on Cook's tours, leading them to the burial places of the Holy Fathers, meeting fair-haired monks in wadis that run between bare mountains and paying them to show tourists inspiring spots bathed in history. Adonsky knew where to find Greek and Roman glass, ancient coins and jewels, angels and saints. He knew the ecstasy of this oppressed land as well as its proud and despondent groans. Evenings he would walk the streets as though enchanted with the pleasant breeze, meet newcomers who spoke of Emancipation, the revival of Hebrew and Zionism. He would discern which way the wind was blowing and respond accordingly, buying land on behalf of the newcomers in spots that were inconceivable, as yet undreamed of, clinging in his heart to one fundamental principle: this people is not being revived, nor is it being built and rebuilt in this harsh land; no pyramids are being inverted, Borochov's economic theories notwithstanding.

We are Jews. The pyramid will be inverted again and break. He knew this bitter land harbored little love for masters with ancient credentials. He believed in land certificates granted by effendis in Beirut with French maidens perched on their laps emptying their pockets. He had no faith in our father Abraham's certificates, mocked the broken dream, a gay dream charged with fury and madness, propelling young people to go to the Galilee to create themselves and their people anew. But he found them land, knowing it would ultimately be for burial rather than life. He knew the Creator to have an affection for dead Jews. And the Creator did, after all, reside in this land, was born here, created here. The land, being in itself the story of His thwarted love, would remain as it had always been, evidence of His eternal vengeance against those who love Him. God would never grant His Jews life in this land where graves are designed to afford a view of the Messiah's approach.

One cannot understand Aunt Shlomzion the Great without understanding Miriam's gentility and frailness or Adonsky's inability to laugh. Adonsky met Herr Wolff among the burial plots. He knew Wolff was no doctor, was aware of his dark designs on him. When World War I broke out and the country was plagued with famine, Herr Wolff took Adonsky under his wing. When the English took over and the Turks as well as their German allies were expelled, Adonsky protected Wolff. Herr Wolff wept when he left the country. He had lived there as a spy for fifty-one years, siring numerous children. He didn't know his sons and daughters, regarding himself as some pagan god scattering seed throughout the land to produce a succession of little gods. It was a splendid moment when he marched himself toward the ship and recited a poem of Hölderlin with tears streaming down his face. Some years later, Herr Wolff returned to settle in Sharona. He was very old when the Nazis rose to power. He detested them and composed letters of indictment, which he sent to Germany. Still, he was expelled by the residents of Sharona and left the country a second time. After taking leave of Shlomzion, who was by then married to Nehemiah and mother of Arpahshad (who fled to the United States where he called himself Arty Brand), Herr Wolff died on the boat.

When he left, Shlomzion said to herself: Once, when the French ship fired five shots that flashed through my hair, a new era was born. That short era, dreary and diffuse, is now at an end and from here on even the disgust is more severe.

Adonsky loved Shlomzion above all else. Miriam was annihilated by blind hate for Adonsky. She didn't die; she simply evaporated. One day they found her bones in her bed. Beside the bed a suitcase was discovered, filled with jewels and vituperative letters addressed to Adonsky. She had been writing them all her life without sending them. Despite her disintegrated state, she was as beautiful as ever when she died. One day the substance that held her together was no longer there and she resembled a Roman perfume bottle—antique, transparent and blue, of the sort brought by Adonsky from Apollonia to enhance his splendid collection of objets d'art—shattered, leaving no trace.

She was just such an object; her beauty was undiminished, continuing to glisten reproachfully, even when she crumbled into dust. She died as stars do in distant galaxies, transformed into anti-matter and consumed so that only her beauty, traced on delicate silken fibers, remained visible.

Savage love can be a treasured jewel; it can be slow death. Miriam was both. Ben-Amram died with her. His name was erased. Rabbi Azulai had already written his books without begging forgiveness from God or the deceased Rabbi. Ben-Amram, too, wrote books written by others before him. Rabbi Azulai never admitted that everything he wrote had already been written by Ben-Amram. Circles are closed in this manner. Miriam died and was buried in the cemetery on Trumpeldor Street.

Many years later Adonsky would be buried beside her in ingenious and impressive ceremony. Miriam was buried furtively, as was her wish. She didn't die, Adonsky said; she simply vanished.

Shlomzion's beauty was as rare as her mother's. Like her, she was thin and charged with fury that combined the emotions of both mother and father. She had charm, captivating and mysterious, that won hearts, though it made many uneasy. She was Adonsky's daughter, his likeness reflected into eternity.

To this day there are several old women (their number is declining) willing to swear that Shlomzion was born in Adonsky's bosom. This is the story that prevailed in Jaffa: Shlomzion was born before Dr. Hissin arrived. She emerged from her mother's womb only to crawl over to Adonsky, who was seated nearby in a brown suit and black hat, enter his body and emerge again, bloodstained, as if wishing to enter the world from inside of Adonsky, her beloved. She hated Miriam from the day of her birth. They did not communicate with each other at all. She never turned to her mother except for various polite exchanges. Miriam was equally contemptuous of the fruit of her belly. She called her daughter Shlomzion, and Shlomzion called her mother Miriam. She was raised by Adonsky. They spent years together in the large room overlooking the sea, dealing with every problem that arose, so that Shlomzion was well versed in her father's affairs even before she could read or write.

When I told Little Mother Shlomzion my wish to write about Shlomzion the Great, she smiled a smile in which one could not detect the sadness of those captivated by Aunt Shlomzion's villainy. She merely pondered the matter intently and said: Me again?

I said: Not you; it's Aunt Shlomzion the Great I'm thinking of. Aunt Shlomit is convinced my plan will avenge itself by destroying those dearest to me, one by one. She said: Tomorrow you'll write a horror story about your daughters.

But neither Mother nor Aunt Shlomit concealed their secret pleasure at the thought that Auntie would finally get her due. If I write the story, Shlomzion the Great will surely not read it.

Nor will her son Arty Brand read it or Amihud Sohlovsky, who anticipates the crumbs of inheritance. Her possible heirs don't read stories, not about themselves or about anyone else. I would read the story to Ben-Amram, Adonsky or Miriam, or to the French officer who fired the five shots that flashed through Shlomzion's hair. But apart from the officer, whose fate I have not followed, all those who really deserve to read the story dwell in dust. Shlomzion the Great doesn't read. Even at her peak she seldom read. Uncle Nehemiah is dead and Little Mother Shlomzion will feel pressured, straining to be amused at those points where compassion repays Aunt Shlomzion the Great for doses of malevolence she conferred on Mother's own sorrowful life.

So this is not a question of vengeance but of research into the nature of ultimate evil, dazzling and seductive.

One week after I told Little Mother Shlomzion about the story brewing in my head, she told me a dream. She had been in the private hospital in north Tel Aviv that day, visiting Shlomzion the Great. It was spring. The day was fragrant and fair. Newspapers reported new adversities: the lira was devaluated; there was violence on the border. Everyone was rushing home, depressed, to watch the news on television. Little Mother Shlomzion left the hospital filled with the presence of Shlomzion the Great, like a clump of venomous thorns. She was making her way down a street flooded by sudden fragrances. The cars stopped for a light on the corner where a giant sycamore tree once stood, the one that ripped my pants whenever I tried, desperately, to read books on the high limbs at its crown. Mother Shlomzion smiled to herself recalling the torn pants, the sticky sycamore fruits smeared on my clothes. This memory had elements of infinite sadness for the sands that were no longer there, the vineyards that had been cut down, the glorious fields circled by cactus fences, replaced by shapeless concrete blocks. Also, she laughed to herself, not without bitterness, remembering Shlomzion's inability to tolerate the fact that I, Little Mother Shlomzion's despicable son, a middle-aged man, had laughed heartily in her room. When? Three days ago. That day was a fine one, too, she thought.

I was visiting with my younger daughter, who wanted to see my funny old aunt. I told her she was not really funny. My little girl said: Not ha-ha funny, but funny in a sad way. We stayed only a few minutes. Shlomzion said: You look bad. . . . Then she turned to Mother. Nehemiah didn't like him at all. Nehemiah was simply polite. He knew how to handle children. Where did you get the foolish notion that Nehemiah cared for Aminadav? He cared only for Shlomzion.

I then reminded Mother that my sister Hamutal was born here, on the second floor, one level below the room we were now in, as was my younger daughter, now present. I was astonished at the tender tears that suddenly overwhelmed me. Remembering the circumstances of my sister's birth, I was restored to a world of sweetness, small-town life, young parents, younger than myself at that moment. I remembered lying in the big bed with my father waiting for the gift from heaven. It was a winter night, with cold winds blowing in from a stormy sea which, in those days, was right under Mother and Father's window. We used to watch the fish jumping just beyond the screened window. Father was snoring and I was dozing. Uncle Abner, who was a night watchman, galloped in suddenly, announcing: Naftali, you have a daughter, and began laughing. When he arrived at the door, Father and I had already fallen off the bed, which had collapsed under us.

Hamutal was born the night Father and I fell out of bed. This is still a very sweet memory and I don't know if the sweetness of that moment derives from the sweet cereal I ate later, or if the reverse is true and the cereal derived its sweetness from that moment. After Uncle Abner went to bring the news to Shlomit, and to run to the hospital with her to see the sister that was born to me, Father got up and stared at me from amidst the ruins of the bed (he looked like a puppet dropped in the middle of a marionette show) and asked what one does with a seven-year-old boy at five-thirty-six in the morning. I said that maybe we should run to Mother first of all. He said: Yes, but she told me to feed you and I am a disciplined person who falls out of beds and makes breakfast for his son. We began laughing again, because we had in fact fallen out of bed a few seconds before Uncle Abner appeared. It was later established that Mother gave birth to Hamutal at precisely that instant, that Uncle Abner had been in the hospital, heard that Mother was about to deliver and, thinking she had already given birth, had run to us and found us falling out of bed. He had then run back to the hospital to be informed that his sister had in fact given birth at the very moment we fell out of bed. Our precious little Hamutal was born, to upset everyone's lives, maybe, or so I would eat Quaker Oats for the first time. Father didn't know how to cook Quaker Oats. But he, of course, refused to appear incompetent before his small son. So he rushed to the kitchen pretending to be an expert and cooked cereal which was the best I ever ate. After that he made my cereal every morning. His formula remained a secret for ten years. He finally taught me the method. I make my daughters cereal now. They lick their dishes clean. Mother tried to learn the method but failed. My wife also failed. It's not the method, Aunt Shlomit says, but the music . . . something added to the water, sugar, butter and oats.

Who was born here? Aunt Shlomzion the Great asked.

Hamutal and also my daughter! I pointed to her, and Mother Shlomzion smiled in a grandmotherly fashion while straightening something on Shlomzion's night table.

Ah, said Aunt Shlomzion the Great, with a grimace the likes of which I had never seen before, such as one might expect to see on someone whose profession it is to climb gallows, or on a cat being trampled. She pointed toward the second floor and said in a voice charged with irritation and disgust: Yes, they're being born there all the time!

Little Mother Shlomzion is in a state of combined glee and melancholy. She wants to grasp the dream. The night was very quiet and full of worry. She fell asleep for an hour and dreamed she was in a room full of mirrors; she saw herself looking different in each one, as if each moment of her life were granted its own mirror. And all of these Little Mother Shlomzions were engrossed in the book written by me, her dear son, the book about Aunt Shlomzion the Great. These little Shlomzions with all their moments reflected in an unending series of mirrors wept as they spoke: Look, a book about a beautiful woman, a book about a beautiful woman! She retorts: Don't write a book about her; don't use your magic to invoke Adonsky. No more destruction! You have been destructive enough. Let them live, God. How have they offended you? Why be vengeful? Aunt Shlomit shares the opinion that writing is a vicious act, inflicting painful vengeance. I, too, am aware that it is suicide and love linked together. I know one writes not about Aunt Shlomzion but about oneself. So that I am writing about myself through this dreadful and inexorably captivating woman, a woman full of vice and evil. And, becoming all the more evil, I am prepared for that single revenge that fulfills some destiny, revenge against myself. Which I deserve.

Can the story of Shlomzion the Great in fact be written? It is too late to retreat, I told Little Mother Shlomzion. My dear Little Shlomzion mends fragments, rescues people who haven't drowned yet, feels such pity for herself that she succeeds in pitying others as well. But vengeance is at hand. The awesome wrath of those rescued against their will.

18

An elderly attorney, grand and imposing, wearing a black suit despite the heat, the beads of sweat soaked up by his heavy clothes, the ruddiness of age on his face . . . He has already phoned in desperation, hoping to learn further details. Shlomzion has outsmarted him. He appeared at Barclays Bank, in all his dignity, only to be turned back like a scolded boy. The bank had been instructed unequivocally to deny him satisfaction. He was seeking the individual who had issued this directive. Would a fine woman like Shlomzion mislead him after forty-seven years of impeccable service? She had abandoned him long ago, though he was unaware of this.

I meet him in the hall of the private hospital in north Tel Aviv. His eyes are vacant like someone hit below the belt who refuses to expose the black-and-blue marks. I remain his enemy. Though he was just thrown out of Shlomzion's room, he observes me sadly, his dull stare framed in silver, a rosy-faced attorney, rejected. Watching a young man race by in a showy sports car, he recalls a time when he used to dash about in his splendid carriage.

But the transition is too swift, his eyes confide, and I will not demean myself before you, young man. He wishes, like everyone trampled by Shlomzion, to understand, to love her wickedness, to scorn her only in the company of those worthy of scorning so marvelous a woman. I am forbidden, absolutely, to scorn Shlomzion in your company, his eyes seem to declare. You are not in that class! You are not in that level of humanity!

I sit in the garden among the geranium bushes. Hamutal has gone up to smile at Shlomzion the Great. The attorney waits for a cab. On the way home he will weep and wipe away the tears. He will phone other elderly attorneys, his cronies from another time, and try to trip them up. He will sink into his old bed, solitary, in a white nightshirt, and die that very night. A year is three hundred and sixty-five dead dogs.

She built a fence around herself. Only occasionally, on Shabbat afternoons when there were no important guests at her house, did she consent to come to us. Mother did her own cooking. On Fridays she would come from work, do the shopping and send me for more: cake from Mendele street, white cheese and butter from the fat man who reeked of beer and sausages, who lived in one of those white houses with red roofs in the German colony near the sycamore tree and the nut store, where that girl—a child, perhaps—whose hair was dark and eyes bright with a meaning apart from its dream, with a delicate air, extraneous and ungenerous, an annoying sort of beauty, a girl in a yellow dress that laced, used to bring me cheese from a room where even in those days one could see pictures of the Führer and feel a deliberate disregard of my past, a violent indifference. The cheese, nonetheless, contained the forgotten softness of even more distant days, of excursions in the fat man's wagon to the Lower Galilee at night with Father singing German songs by the light of the moon, she and I casting smooth pebbles into a ravine enveloped in darkness that was utterly bright, illuminating itself; grains of sand in her hair and laughter while Father recited poetry and the German cursed in hilarious German-Arabic, the horse snorting in the background—and over all the Galilean night, composed of essences that touch but never meet.

Later Mother cooks on all the burners, using up the wicks. Father reproaches her. He is drying the glasses, shining them carefully. He breaks one and exclaims ceremoniously: Behold you are betrothed unto me. She, poor thing, shouts: Who betrothed? We won't have any glasses left and Shlomzion is coming! She begins to cry and, meaning to amuse her, he tells us for the hundred and first time how the Americans and the Chinese go about digging a tunnel. The Americans take a hundred engineers and put them at their desks. Then they bring two groups of workers who begin to dig, having calculated that on the twentieth of June, a Sunday, at four o'clock, the groups will meet and there will be a tunnel. Whereas the Chinese bring a million people to one side of the mountain and another million to the other side to begin digging, and if and when they meet there is a tunnel; if not there are two tunnels! At this point there is nothing to be done. He laughs and she doesn't. The glass is gone. Shlomzion is on the way. She will arrive the following afternoon.

The food is ready. Everyone is expectant. Father will spend the morning on the balcony, reading Goethe, gazing at the sea, while Mother makes further preparation, adds final touches, tastes and seasons. Everything is reàdy. At twelve-thirty in the afternoon, before the news followed by Mr. Kapilowitz's analysis predicting the precise timing of the surrender of the evil Nazi forces, they arrive—Nehemiah smiling, Aunt Shlomzion the Great tired and harassed under her enormous hat. She is full of compassion for all of us, consoling Mother with a glance filled with retroactive understanding as she points to Father on the balcony and exclaims: You make your bed, then you lie in it! Father retorts, laughing: Xanthippe is here! Nehemiah's laughter is unduly loud and Shlomzion says: Maybe we should speak German, since Naftali doesn't know Hebrew. I say that if I knew Hebrew as well as Father I would get "very good" rather than "improving" on my report card, to which she says: Yes, but once a German, always a German. Though we know this doesn't apply to Father we don't protest for fear of fanning the fire.

Silence. We listen to news on the Voice of Jerusalem and to Mr. Kapilowitz. After which we are surrounded by outbursts of cantorial singing from every direction and Father raises his voice in *Aïda*. The neighborhood twins pee their names in the strip of sand between our house and the sea which can still be seen from our balcony. Aunt Shlomit looks out from her balcony, beyond the fermentation and the test tubes filled with mossy specimens, bewailing the futility of her passing days. At which point Aunt Shlomzion the Great has her say: Well, riffraff sticks with riffraff. It's always been that way—in Jaffa, too. I remember Adonsky saying to me; Tell me who your neighbors are and I'll tell you who you are. Still, I'm not complaining. Yes, yesterday it was difficult. Nehemiah didn't feel well, as usual. I took the three pills today and he suddenly decided to sleep. I say to him: Nehemiah, we're going to Little Shlomzion today because I wanted to, and he, poor thing, gets dressed grumbling all the time. Look at him, he'll soon die of starvation. But does anyone care?

We finally sat down to eat and Mother served the soup. I waited. Nehemiah had already swallowed two spoonsful and smiled. Father broke a piece of *hallah* with extreme concentration. Mother got up, sat down, got up again. Hamutal in the high chair, laughing with her mouth full of grapes, wet herself.

Aunt Shlomzion took a taste, kept the soup in her mouth, and for several anguished moments charged with self-sacrifice, unspoken implications, and bottomless torment, she remained suspended between life and death. Finally, she swallowed the soup, grimacing like an injured baby. She left the spoon in the bowl, dried her face with a napkin and adopted an attitude of menacing silence. Father began eating heartily. But Nehemiah stopped. She said: Yessss, drawing out the *s*. Then she grew pale, seemed about to faint and revived. She said: The help today, that's the problem. There's not much they know, and there are those who know what not to know to a glorious degree! They are as plentiful as pigeons. They take over the household because their masters become chauffeurs for the British or something similar, selling themselves for a few cents. They're beginning to live in houses and Lord only knows what they think. Now they cook the soup and what comes out? Poor Little Shlomzion is the victim. I have to find her new help. If I live and manage to make it home to salvage my own skin, which will be shriveled as the night in some ugly world by tomorrow . . . And what will come of it!

She didn't ask; she asserted.

We all stared at her. Hamutal chirped: Aunt Shlomshyon, Aunt Shlomshyon, the tow dumped over the moon! Fishie in a dishie! Fish, dish, squish.

Father was quick to explicate: The fish went squish in the dish. Nehemiah felt he had been rescued, and gulped the soup down. He didn't look up at Mother, who was trapped in the rapid flow of Aunt Shlomzion's words. Father added: Hamutal's words are still all mixed up. She can't say *k* or *g*. She says *ting* for *king*. She says *dumb* for *gum*. What does the duck say, sweetheart?

Twack, twack, says my sweet little sister Hamutal.

Nehemiah laughs, poor thing, and finishes his soup. Shlomzion, who has eaten only that one dreadful spoonful, says: She's clever like her father! Mother, trying to salvage the remnants, says: I cooked it myself, Shlomzion, especially for you!

I love the soup very very much, says Shlomzion. It's truly excellent. But, unfortunately, I had a late breakfast. You are a very fine cook for someone who spends the day doing other things. I hope there is no chicken. They're so tough nowadays.

She didn't even try the chicken. She had so many bitter words to say. We all ate the chicken and the words. Afterward we sat on the balcony watching the sea turn blue, then violet, the clouds trailing above, the birds hovering over the Muslim cemetery. Aunt Shlomzion didn't know that Assam Kassani was still buried there. It was later, ten years later, that his grave was moved.

19

Shlomzion sees birds through the window of her hospital room. Little Mother Shlomzion insists that Shlomzion the Great never spoke of birds before. Now she observes them hours on end beyond the two images stationed on her bureau: Adonsky, Captain of the World, and Nehemiah, dressed as a clown. Aunt Shlomzion began looking at birds at the age of seventy-six. Very nearly seventy-seven, I corrected. Little Mother Shlomzion confirmed this point in astonished elation. The stylish doctor is not interested in birds. He is examining a feeble woman and fails to notice birds rustling in her eyes, like in the dying eyes of Assam Kassani so many years ago, or in Adonsky's metaphysical concerns when he grew very old. Shlomzion may also be approaching the moment of rest she so deserves.

I myself, having begun with the wish to understand Shlomzion, modify my dismay with glimpses of select moments, seeking, in the very least, to understand them or to render them in appropriate form. The moment of the five French shells in her hair, moments of great gloom or ecstasy . . . For there are elements of charm and grace in this mistress of evil, daughter of Jezebel, Adonsky's mate in his dream, Miriam's daughter gaining support from a Sidonite Jezebel all those years.

Something in her eyes is beginning to fade. The moment she discovered birds and began chirping *tsif-tsif* at them, I noticed that vast secret quality that used to enervate and enthrall us at one and the same time beginning to dim. She sits in her bed, which costs her twelve thousand lirot a month. Birds flutter near her window, coming to eat crumbs tossed out by the nurse in accordance with her surprising instruction. She pinches her pretty mouth, a blend of silk with stone, and coos *tsif-tsif!* But the light in her eyes is extinguished or has, perhaps, extinguished something else, something that seems so massive in its absence, so shocking as it expires!

I was at Aunt Shlomit's house with Mother Shlomzion trying to clarify various matters pertaining to Aunt Shlomzion the Great: three who are not among her heirs, three who submit to her. We decided to write a letter to Arty Brand. Shlomit refused. Mother was uneasy, so I wrote it myself. I wrote that Shlomzion was suddenly extinguished. That one day she shut her eyes and when she woke up they were different. She no longer has bitter words, only complaints and accusations: that we refuse to cover her at night; that we are concealing Mother's new husband. And that's all. Listen, I wrote to him, she no longer tells me how bad I look. She doesn't accuse me of stealing stamps; she doesn't even remember where she put the keys to her house. I suggest you come. I know, I wrote, what you feel and what your life has been like, how much you suffered because of her. I know you are excluded from her will, though I have never seen any one of her five wills. But, I wrote, she is your mother, the only mother you ever had, and you ought to see her. It's your duty to come, Art, even if you call the visit by another name and try to find an executor who will salvage some of what you deserve. Nehemiah's bonds, in the very least, belong to you. And the house? What will become of the house? Art did not answer immediately. I wrote a friend asking that he try to speak to him. The friend wrote me that Art seemed to be in bad shape; that he and his wife had separated and he was trying to rescue his children from what he termed: my mother's curse. Art, the same friend wrote me, is hanging out with a young girl of twenty-two, twenty-four years younger than Art. He calls himself Arpahshad in odd moments of emotion and sadness, wrapped in melancholy, attempting, like his mother, to fish himself up from the depths of a mirror framed in gold or a stage flooded with glittering lights. I said to myself: in total contrast to his mother, perhaps deliberately so, he loves the world in Technicolor and hates himself in black-and-white.

I understand. Fifteen years ago Aunt Shlomzion decided to visit her son in the United States. She wrote him, outlining in great detail just what it was that impelled her to forgo her sense of propriety and come to him. She wanted to find out if it was possible to rescue him, to meet her grandchildren in order to decide whether to leave them the books inherited from her father, as well as several pieces of furniture. She hoped to see why he persisted in regarding a Japanese whore as his wife and why he saw fit to bring more mongoloids into the world.

My sister Hamutal was in the United States at the time. She was traveling from San Francisco to New York and was staying with Art in Chicago. She found him in a depressed state. The children were huddled around the picture of Grandma as Art tried to explain that Grandma, this entity speaking a foreign tongue, was to arrive in a few days and that they were expected to behave in accordance with instructions he would issue. The children were afraid of her. They didn't know her, but their faces made it plain that they were not looking forward to the meeting. I am taking care to use my words discreetly.

One of Art's daughters was, truly, very sick, though extremely beautiful and well developed physically. Her name was Melissanda. She was the absolute and inexplicable image of Shlomzion and of Miriam, Shlomzion's mother. She was the third link in the chain, the consummate likeness of those that preceded her. I once told Art that I never knew anyone to so totally resemble her grandmother. He asked: Wwwwwwhy? . . . And shuddered. I drank some water after his extended why, and replied: Because! Had you seen the picture of your Grandmother, Miriam, as I saw it, you might understand what a miracle it is. Some old man from Hebron was guarding it like an amulet. He died clutching it in his hand. They said he was a wise and learned scholar, the son of a famous rabbi; that he was humiliated by Adonsky once, remaining mute for five years; that he married, bore sons and daughters and fled from Hebron during the great massacre, but was never parted from the wretched picture of Miriam, which he was forbidden to carry; that it dangled from his neck sometimes like a charm, at other times like a private slaughter knife. Had you but seen it, I said to Art, who was Arpahshad, my cousin, you would understand what a miracle it is.

But Art was an expert in securities, not miracles. He expressed no interest in the history of Miriam's family or of Rabbi Ben-Amram. He could scarcely speak Hebrew. He had fought for his daughter's health and failed. She was a very violent girl, extremely beautiful, an exquisite embarrassment. He had been battling her disease, losing his wife in the process. His business failed; he lost his money, struggled to start anew and succeeded. Financing himself once again in obscure corners, he was comforted. In the United States, Arty Brand was considered a sober man. A brilliant card player who gambled in securities and bonds, he became a senior member of a Chicago firm that had never hired a Jew before. Not even a converted Jew, he told me in great excitement. He spoke fluent English and relived the story of America with such zeal that he wept a few tears when recalling the shot that killed Lincoln more than a hundred years ago.

But in Hebrew he always stuttered.

When he met Israelis or members of the family, his entire countenance would be transformed; his eyes would be coated by a thick fog that suggested dead vapors. He would immediately begin stammering and make scornful references to the Land of Israel or the State. As Shlomzion once remarked in a moment of great excitement, he was the end.

Despite all his efforts, Melissanda did not recover. He now knows how to live with the tragedy. Shlomzion says it all derives from the genes; i.e., from Simha, my grandfather. She can even prove it. Take Little Shlomzion's son Aminadav, she used to say. Do you know anyone more disturbed? Living off others, destroying families with great relish. Ugly. A father to daughters who are not really his.

I remain silent.

My cousin's divorced wife is doing well at the University in Massachusetts and may even feel sorry for him. They lived together about twenty-one years. Shlomzion's poison struck her so deeply that she was compelled to leave him. One night, when he was drunk, Arty called the mother of his four children a Japanese whore.

When Shlomzion announced her intention to visit her son, he was still married to Sandra, his wife and the mother of his children. My sister Hamutal, who spent a couple of days in Chicago en route from San Francisco to New York, had a pleasant enough time at Art's house. Shlomzion's letter arrived while she was in Chicago.

In her letter Shlomzion clearly assumed that someone, meaning Arpahshad himself, would be waiting for her at the airport in New York, that from there he would take her to Chicago. I am likely to get confused, she wrote, and board a plane for Russia, or some such place, and from there who knows.

Art was busy and harassed. He claimed he couldn't go to New York to meet his mother for several reasons. First, he said, it's nonsense. She'll arrive on El Al, get off the plane, walk a short distance to another plane, the one with yellow stewardesses, and arrive at the Chicago airport. Why should he travel to New York to wait for a grown woman who has traveled outside of her country on countless other occasions? All this to lead her from one flight to another?

Art was in a tight financial spot at that point. The expense seemed excessive to him.

He was afraid to be alone with his mother.

Hamutal made a somewhat odd proposal, for which she paid dearly. Out of consideration for her cousin (as well as deep feminine sensibility and the ability not to complicate matters) she would be willing to welcome Shlomzion in New York, to accompany her to the United flight and dispatch her to her son.

Arty Brand was pleased and thanked Hamutal. He stuttered at great length in a valiant attempt to express his pleasure in Hebrew. He switched to English and, in a succession of syncopated sentences, recalled memories of her childhood as though describing a menacing volcano made of sugar.

Hamutal took leave of Sandra and Art and flew to New York. On a stormy Sunday, amid winds and heavy downpour, she went from one Chinese restaurant to another, studying the future with waning concentration (thanks to the wine), comparing the terse messages in the fortune-cookie papers. She learned that a long and fascinating life awaited her; that she would travel throughout the wide world; that despite her travails only good things were in store for her in the future. Someone, in fun, even revealed to her on paper rolled in a cookie that he was trapped in a wild orgy on a certain street in Canton, and implored: Please, come quickly and save my capitalist organ from the red scissors that snip oh so mercilessly.

She laughed and drank mint tea. Then, in the heavy downpour and fierce wind, after six Chinese dinners, she went to the airport.

A few minutes before the plane arrived, the rain suddenly stopped. Something strange happened to that rain, Hamutal told me later. She went outside, and while the six (sick?) Chinese dinners talked to each other in her stomach, she addressed herself to the rain: Please, pretty please, stop! (She regressed in honor of her aunt, overcome with the awe that engulfs us all just before landing within striking range of Aunt Shlomzion the Great.) She said: Pretty please, stop now and don't irritate Auntie!

I didn't even shout at the rain, Hamutal recounted. I merely whispered.

Suddenly, in a rapid switch, like the action of the machine

Hamutal pores over hours on end doing film cuts, the rain stopped.

The plane landed in a freshly bathed field under almost clear skies. Scarlet twilight lit the corners of the sky. The afterglow would soon begin pouring golden light over the open spaces; then darkness would descend, embracing everything.

Hamutal awaits the flight. She has made the acquaintance of an aged pilot drinking whiskey at the bar, of the stationmaster, who allows her out on the airfield, and of two synthetic stewardesses molded in plastic. Hamutal is busy soothing the cuisines of Shanghai and Canton, vying inside her for the birthright. The plane touches down and approaches in air cleansed by rain, framed by a stunning display of leaping lights and shining runways that darken suddenly.

When Shlomzion the Great, in a splendid wool suit and hair fastened with a hundred thousand little pins, discovered Hamutal she began shrieking. The airport held its breath. A woman lovely as a bird was shrieking in the roadway illuminated by plane lights that erupt and disappear in the dusky sky, surrounded by the thunderous roar of jets.

But Shlomzion's voice prevails.

Where is Arpahshad? she shrieks. Where? So it wasn't convenient for him? Why you? Who asked you? Who sent you? Who are you anyway? Why are you pursuing me? Get out of here, you ugly thing. Like mother, like daughter. I suppose she's here, too, stirring up a revolution to get at the little money I still have! Go away!

Hamutal tries to calm down. She takes a pill. They work fast, the doctor had said. He didn't know he was giving her an anti-Shlomzion pill. The Chinese dinners and the double Librium begin to do their furtive work. Rain is waiting in the sky. It will fall again when Shlomzion takes off.

But she won't take off.

She will wait until her miserable son appears, she says, turning to the bystanders crowded around her. She is holding a small suitcase, studying the luggage as it moves along the conveyor belt, determined not to allow some scoundrel to steal the little (nearly nothing) she possesses in the bitter and hostile world that has always engulfed her. She shouts: Bring him here! What does he mean? Who is this little fool anyway? She flings herself down on the bench between the plane and the passenger wing, refusing to move. Hamutal's eyes fill with blinding tears. She soothes, cajoles, tries explaining, not explaining. People wonder, smile, watch with a mixture of pity and suspicion. Shlomzion bursts in on the stationmaster. She demands to speak with the manager, the mayor, insists she knows the President. After all, she was once in the diplomatic corps. She knows all the right people! She will sit there until she gets satisfaction.

She will not leave.

The El Al manager is a mature and gracious man. He is accustomed to the bizarre and is paid to deal with it. He, too, tries to calm her. She stares at him, then asks: What's your name?

Hamutal tries to pick up the suitcase. Shlomzion slaps her hand: Don't steal it! You and your mother! Simha's flesh and blood! You would trade an airport for a washbasin. You could work for my cleaning lady, do her laundry with bleach and bluing in a tub of hot water. You have Naftali's hands! What are you doing sidling up to Adonsky's daughter? You didn't even know him. . . . Listen, I know your name, she said, turning sharply to the station manager.

He said: Madam, come to the office and we'll work it all out. Every problem has a solution!

What did you say your name was, handsome? she asked.

Max Evron, he replied.

Max Evron? She articulates the words slowly. Her face begins to beam. A professional sort of glow, true to character, veils her eyes for a minute: You? Whom are you trying to impress? You are Max's son. . . . Your name, without an evil eye, is Ahiasaf Labour.

The station manager blushes. To be born with a name like that . . .

She sizes him up. Listen here, you think I don't know you?

Your Aunt Ketzia came to Nehemiah's funeral to get a free ride to the cemetery and to ask your father rhetorical and unethical questions: Loves me, loves me not! . . . I know you all. Listen here, Labour . . .

He whispers: Here I am known as Max Evron!

So be it! I'm not moving. The adopted daughter of my poor husband's adopted sister is here to lead me astray. You must save me!

He apologizes. He is being paged. The walkie-talkie in his hand is beeping urgently. After the commotion and curiosity all is calm, all is bright.

The crowd vanishes, melting into the illuminated warmth of the airport. Only poor Hamutal remains. Shlomzion and Hamutal make their way toward the waiting area. They sit silently on a secluded bench bathed in fluorescent light. Hamutal says: Listen, Auntie, Art couldn't come. Melissanda is in bad shape. He would have come despite everything if not for the fact that I was flying to New York and he thought—

He's not capable of thinking, so don't you tell me stories!

He thought, Hamutal repeats, that it wouldn't be terrible if some member of the family was here to greet you. Look, I'm only taking you to a plane a hundred and fifty meters from here. It leaves for Chicago in ten minutes. You'll soon land in Chicago and fall right into Art's arms.

His name is Arpahshad!

Arp's arms.

Say Arpahshad!

Arpahshad!

It's not good enough for them? They're assimilated. You know what happened to the assimilationists? Hitler killed them off.

Those who refused to assimilate were killed too, says Hamutal.

Shlomzion scrutinizes her carefully, wondering what this child is doing here. Lord, she is no longer a child. They do grow up! They will soon be bearing children!

She says: They're assimilated. And you listen: I'm going right back. I'm going home!

No, you can't do that. He's waiting for you.

Listen here, I'm going. She gets up. Hamutal tries to sit her down. It is no use. She makes a frenzied scene, wringing her hands, weeping, collecting a new audience, agonizing before her public. Then she sits down again. Hamutal runs to bring her water, then tea. She is paying for Shlomzion, who requests a sandwich, tastes it, flings it in the trash declaring it abominable. Utterly abominable! Then they pick up the suitcases and begin walking. Again she sinks into a chair. It's late. The plane has already taken off.

Hamutal deliberates. Should she call Art? She decides not to. Instead, she sends a telegram with the new flight time, runs to exchange the tickets and checks the flight information carefully. Aunt Shlomzion thinks: Is he trying to kill me? She buys insurance listing King Ahab as beneficiary, Samaria as his address. It is signed *Queen of Samaria*. She doesn't consider this funny and asks Hamutal to explain her strange noises. When Hamutal describes them as laughter, she insists it isn't funny. No one laughs in my earshot, she says, marching quickly (with Hamutal staggering behind) to another counter, where she samples a sandwich, then throws it away and graciously allows Hamutal (who is almost out of cash) to pay. She announces she will fly to Chicago but only to teach her son a lesson he will never forget. Then, on the bench they are occupying, she suddenly exclaims: Chicago? That's the Wild West with all those anti-Semites, no?

Hamutal explains that the Wild West lies beyond Chicago.

What about all the riots, the outlaws and that sheriff? What's his name again? Gary Cooper?

He's an actor, says Hamutal, beginning to crumble. Her mind is distraught, her eyes shredded. She longs for the redeeming flight.

I must be careful, says Shlomzion tearfully, wiping her eyes, her bereavement and the theft perpetrated by her son. I have one son, she says, and he refuses to see me. I have only one son.

You had two sons, no?

Yes.

I have one who refuses to see me. I come from a distance of a hundred million light-years and he turns me down. He was in my belly. His father refused to know him until he was two. They called him "that one." The boy is ungrateful. He doesn't know how much I sacrificed for him. I almost lost Adonsky's sympathy. His own father refused to acknowledge him. The entire family, including your mother, refused to acknowledge him. He grew up in my room. I was besieged in there with him, like in a fortress. They wanted to steal him from me, she said, piercing the room with her bitter sobs. Now he despises me, sends me bizarre messengers. . . . Do you know what? I will go to him but only if he agrees to become a Jew again!

But, Shlomzion, he is a Jew, Hamutal protests.

Are you sure? Because I wouldn't go to Greece. Nehemiah was once invited to Greece and I wouldn't go. They're evil there, every last one. You know about the Greeks. Hannah and her seven martyred sons . . . Antiochus. It's hard to be a Jew.

Yes, Hamutal replies.

Nor would I go to Persia. What's Purim all about? To remind us of those scoundrels. You remember Haman and his wicked sons—Vysata, the youngest? One can't be too careful. You're sure Chicago is all right?

One hundred percent, said Hamutal.

She finally flew to Chicago. Hamutal was alone. Her head throbbed miserably. She thought: That woman! Her eccentric words are so careless and unplanned. She tries to reach others with spears sharp as razors, to touch their inner core, to subjugate them to her thoughts. She knows that inane words, ordered and rhythmic, mouthed wickedly, tempered with sweet stupidity, have a profound effect, and resound—as in the case of saints, innocents, masters of style, witch doctors and charismatic leaders.

I told Hamutal about the Englishman who said oversimplification was a mark of tyranny! Shlomzion is a captivating and monstrous tyrant.

20

Aminadav was ten and a half at the time (ten-thirty, Naftali would say). One day he received a letter from Aunt Shlomzion the Great inviting him to visit her. It was a hot summer day. He rode his red Peugeot and watched the other kids on their Raleighs, a gleam in their eye that was sporting, seductive, menacing. He was thinking: why am I the one with a French bike, a red Peugeot, rather than a Raleigh? Followed by: but why be like all the others? Way back in those sweet days being like the others was, however, a first commandment. He rode to Rothschild Boulevard.

A hot afternoon. The sea breeze begins to blow. He arrives at Shlomzion's. Nehemiah is off somewhere. In the house across the way Mr. Moehl's daughter plays the piano. Chopin. Her lovely hands strike the yellowed keys against the backdrop of a fireplace lined with shiny blue ceramic tiles and a painting of the Western Wall. Adina Moehl's brother is playing tennis in the yard with a red-faced boy in a foreign shirt.

Shlomzion invites him to drink some juice. Aminadav is

baffled. Why did Aunt Shlomzion invite him? Why is she offering him juice? Then she begins, deviously, to lead him around the mulberry bush, as Father would say, and finally descends (one might say pounces) on him with the penetrating question that seems to have been occupying her for over two months: What present does Little Mother Shlomzion intend to bring to Yaira's wedding? Aminadav pretends not to know. Not yet. He is considering whether or not to pass on the information, what value it could have, why she is so eager to know.

Yaira is Shlomzion's niece. Though she has not been on speaking terms with Yaira's father since 1917, she does somehow accept Yaira.

Yaira is not especially attractive or gifted, Aunt Shlomzion says, nor is she even a recognized descendant of Adonsky. But she did return to her homeland of her own free will and is now marrying a local boy. Adonsky is making her a wedding in his splendid house across from Shlomzion's.

Aminadav does not know what present Little Mother Shlomzion has decided to bring. But he doesn't impart even this information lightly. He considers the possibility of inventing something, a way to test Auntie's response before divulging the truth. He has already learned on his own the verbal acrimony of the beautiful woman who lives in this cold house and addresses him as Simha, after a grandfather he never knew at all. He knows, even though he is only ten-thirty, that it is best to curb one's tongue in the vicinity of Shlomzion, adding to himself: the Great. Not merely because she is a few years older than Little Mother Shlomzion, but because he is conscious of the fact that she is, indeed, Great. He is aware of her power, the ability to name things, then set their price. She is some sort of giant priestess, he told a friend one evening as they walked along the Yarkon River, she with her bicycle and he with his.

Mother is buying Yaira skates, he told Aunt Shlomzion.

Shlomzion gazed at him intently, weighing his words.

She knew Mother was not about to buy skates for Yaira, who was being married in Adonsky's house. But she knew that if

Aminadav said skates, it was a sign that Mother Shlomzion intended to buy an expensive present, for what could be more impressive than skates to a street urchin like Aminadav, a waif from an immigrant camp wearing a blue uniform, taken in by all those Communistic follies?!

Ah, Shlomzion said. Skates. That's splendid, Ami. Then I can buy her a collar. Aminadav was silent. He knew collars were for dogs. Shlomzion was not known as a great dog lover. Rex's death remained imprinted on her. As Aminadav saw it, she had murdered Rex and Arpahshad's stutter was not hard to account for. But he understood, having always lived with people who grappled with Shlomzion the Great, that if she said collar it was a sign she was considering something conspicuous, something that would be sure to overshadow Mother's gift.

At home he related exactly what had happened. Mother Shlomzion asked numerous questions. She wanted to know precisely what Shlomzion the Great had said, her tone of voice, how much time elapsed before she responded to his words and exactly how she said collar. Did she say buy a collar or buy her a collar? Was she sitting or standing when she said what she said?

Aunt Shlomit came running. Abner had gone to Haifa. She was breathless. She asked Aminadav to describe at exactly what point Shlomzion had said a collar. Was it before or after the juice? Did she blink a little when he said Mother is buying Yaira skates or did she stand up and begin muttering? Were her eyes cold or warm, and what exactly did she say when she offered him juice?

The interrogation lasted about an hour. Then Aunt Shlomit and Mother Shlomzion secluded themselves in a room. They whispered interminably and concluded that Aunt Shlomzion, upon hearing the word skates, inferred that Mother was planning to buy Yaira a lamp. (They told Father this later, and, unable to contain himself, he laughed aloud and disclosed all to Aminadav.)

Why a lamp?

Because, Aunt Shlomit reasoned, Shlomzion of course didn't believe for a moment that Aminadav knew exactly what Mother

Shlomzion intended to buy. If he knew, he would have said something clear, even if, as one assumes, he meant to lie. So that he definitely did not know. In that case, what is it that he didn't know? He didn't know whether she planned to buy a bracelet, a gold clock or furniture. Adonsky wouldn't permit any member of Simha's family to buy his granddaughter furniture. But, on the other hand, he would be as unwilling to accept a small present, a mere symbol of a present on his granddaughter's behalf (and would, undoubtedly, circulate slanderous rumors about it that would spread with demonic speed). What was left? Furniture—no. A gold bracelet—no. If Mother was planning anything of that sort, Aminadav would be aware of it (as meetings with jewelers create a stir) and would have said a bicycle rather than skates. For something involving gold would stimulate a deep acquisitive sense in him, an appetite stifled by his pioneering youth movement dedicated to the redemption of Israel through a new egalitarian life guided by Spartan ideals. If this repressed acquisitive feeling inherent in us all was indeed aroused, Aunt Shlomit reasons, he would then have said a bicycle. Who doesn't know that all he dreams of is a black Raleigh bicycle to replace the red Peugeot which was once stolen from him and returned immediately with an implied apology: you call this a bike? All the other kids have Raleighs and Raleighs are the best. What use is this Peugeot bicycle anyway?

Aunt Shlomit, who made all these calculations, said that the word skates conveyed to Aunt Shlomzion the Great that the present did not involve gold; that, on the other hand, it wasn't a piece of furniture, but was more likely something that glitters, though it is not used for seating, standing or reclining—three positions in which skates are not useful. All this considered, what is the point of skates?

In short, a lamp would be Aunt Shlomzion's leading hypothesis.

A telephone conversation the following day convinced Aminadav how clever poor Aunt Shlomit really was. Shlomzion the Great called to inquire if Naftali had recovered from diphtheria.

Little Mother Shlomzion said he had recovered and was feeling better, though it was three and a half years ago, in the winter, not the summer, that he was sick.

Aunt Shlomzion the Great didn't even respond to the delicate intimation. She muttered something about diseases brought into the country by the Germans, and added: They think the name Arpahshad isn't good enough; well, what about Bag-Bag?

Who?

Bag-Bag, my aunt replied, astounding Mother with her knowledgeability. He was Tana's father! You never heard of him?

No, said Little Mother Shlomzion.

The point is that Bag-Bag is no less funny than the lamps one buys in the Bezalel Market!

They don't sell lamps in the Bezalel Market, Mother said cautiously but with ardor. She added: But why this talk about a lamp all of a sudden?

Listen here, Shlomzion, said Shlomzion the Great. Don't try bringing in a truckload of presents. It won't impress Adonsky, nor will it affect the inheritance I intend to leave you someday. Don't try to overwhelm the little virgin. She's sweet enough, but stupid like my son's grandfather on his father's side, an individual with whom you, perhaps, were unacquainted because he never tried—and you may well be the only girl in all of Tel Aviv and Jaffa who can honestly make the claim—to make out with you!

To do what?

Make out, my aunt said, her sharp voice ringing with laughing horror, yet never quite laughing. To make out; seduce! And if you are trying to outwit Adonsky, a lamp won't sweep Yaira off her feet when she stands under the wedding canopy, nor will anyone else be overly excited. Adonsky, for instance, has given her a fine house on Karl Netter Street, with three rental apartments, all in her name. She can live on the income when her foolish husband dies or disappears, as many husbands do. He might become German and engage in espionage on behalf of Goethe or Beethoven like someone whose name happens to be

Naftali, who calls me Xanthippe but doesn't know what I have in store for him!

Whose husband? Mother Shlomzion was stunned.

The husband she is marrying the day after tomorrow! Shlomzion shrieked. The new husband who will do for a while, until Adonsky finds Yaira a more suitable mate. He yielded, you know. She talks about love as if she were me, or someone who knows what it means. Adonsky said: So what; let it be. But the house is in her name. Legally. With an explicit clause forbidding her to transfer ownership. You might as well know.

But why a lamp, my mother asked innocently. What do you have in mind? I wasn't planning to buy a lamp!

Then I suppose you're buying skates, said Aunt Shlomzion the Great. And she slammed down the phone.

Mother Shlomzion bought a phonograph for Yaira. No one had thought of this. Mother mortgaged eight paychecks to buy the phonograph. But the impact was tremendous! Shlomzion the Great bought a small table in the Bezalel Market, had a carpenter attach a pole to it from which an elderly electrician suspended a light fixture. It became necessary to hide the lamp not only because of its bizarre and dim beauty, but also because of its inadequate wiring, which Aunt Shlomit said could transmit a fatal shock even if one merely looked at it.

The phonograph received an ovation. Yaira's husband danced around it as if it were an Indian totem. Yaira turned the switch. Someone brought a record and two old favorites resounded throughout the room.

It was an absolute wonder.

Naftali tried to prevail upon Yaira to come home and choose some Monteverdi, but Shlomzion the Great had already warned the young groom that Naftali was a German spy who begins his operation with gifts of records and concludes by sending reports to Berlin. I am familiar with these spies, she said. Ask Adonsky. He once had a bosom pal called Herr Wolff. He divulged the precise location of Wagner's factory to the French, who then attacked it, firing shots that flashed through my hair.

That, of course, was before I had heard the story about the five shells in Shlomzion's hair. But I knew one thing and I said it: Why would a German spy transmit information about a German factory to the French when he is at war with them?

They were always anti-Semites, Aunt Shlomzion retorted. All of them. Just like the Persians and the Greeks.

Aminadav came to the wedding on his bicycle. He wore a blue shirt and shorts. Chandeliers glistened in the vestibule. Waiters in white uniforms carried trays laden with sandwiches and glittering wine goblets. The house looked like a palace, elegant suits, long gowns trailing across the marble floor. Everything he read in books about the declining world he was battling with a blue work shirt and a Peugeot bicycle unfolded before his very eyes, in all its glory, right here in Tel Aviv.

All this was grotesque against a backdrop of sand dunes and vineyards inhabited by little foxes. The orchestra played, the guests danced waltzes and tangos. Aminadav stood observing, unnoticed, like the end of a cigarette flicked away in error. He gazed at them, thinking: Do I really see what I see?

Children have the capacity to think of themselves in the third person, to wonder if they see what they see. They have certain basic qualities, force, control, love, whose tangibility seems baffling. The house was humming. British officers were there in white uniforms adorned with medals and decorations. There were wealthy merchants from Jaffa, Jerusalem and Trans-Jordan, even from Beirut. Black limousines lined the street. The drivers were playing cards in the boulevard. Tel Aviv's first and foremost citizens arrived, the delicate scent of mothballs clinging to their suits and to the wrinkled hats they dug out of trunks for the occasion. Adonsky looked radiant. The bride's father was searching everywhere for Shlomzion, but she evaded him. Nehemiah drank white wine and played chess with an Englishman, a top official of either this government or Trans-Jordan. Yaira was very beautiful. She wore a simple white silk dress, smooth against her body, suggesting delicate curves, sweet and hidden. Aminadav, in his short pants, blue shirt and unkempt hair, could not avert his eyes from this vision. Mother was celebrating the triumph of the phonograph. Shlomzion went from person to person telling how Mother stole it from Mr. Dizengoff, the Mayor, who was slightly drunk at that point and was stroking Yaira's black hair with excessive fervor. She was very pale. Her eyes were fixed on her young husband.

Mr. Dizengoff said he didn't own a phonograph, nor had he ever owned one. But Shlomzion the Great succeeded in arousing the interest of several Arab gentlemen and one Englishman. The English gentlewoman in their company jumped up suddenly and ran, as if smitten, toward a waiter carrying drinks. She seized two glasses of champagne and gulped them down. She was pale, but the color flowed into her cheeks.

Yaira's husband passed from person to person, exclaiming: I have a phonograph.

He was drunk.

He didn't realize he was really being married.

In the morning he had gone to Natanya where he gulped down a medicinal bottle and sat on the beach weeping. After which he reflected: Where is there a party today? He remembered Adonsky and headed his way, to the gala affair with an orchestra and champagne where, coming upon some friends, he thought he was performing in a school play.

He thought he was playing the groom, with Yaira as the bride, Adonsky as Adonsky and the Rabbi playing Rabbi.

Yaira was crying under the veil.

Her husband would wake up in the morning and discover this was not a school play; he has debts, a wife and Adonsky is on his back. Yaira knew he would be her first husband. She would love the second one more. Still, she wished the first one would love her, too.

Yaira was starved for love. Later, she would know many men, all of whom would try to seduce her for the sole purpose of convincing her to think, throughout her life, that she deserved a little love from every male. She was a very beautiful girl, exceedingly corrupt and exceedingly innocent.

To this day she lives in her house on Karl Netter Street. She is lonely. She never visits Shlomzion in the hospital. She despises Shlomzion. Shlomzion passed on the names of all of her lovers to each of her three husbands. As Shlomzion explained to Yaira, she believed they should all know about each other, since they were, somehow, related.

This is Yaira's first marriage. She looks radiant and melancholy. She was not at all a virgin, Shlomzion intimated to Mother.

Shlomzion the Great knew even this.

Yaira was the image of her father, who searched for Shlomzion in all the stairwells, mumbling agitatedly in English, drinking too much and, at the end of the evening, attempting to make out with the High Commissioner's wife only to be bounced by three gorillas, who were guarding her in a manner that was not at all amiable or tolerant.

All his life Aminadav would remember the alien splendor, all the more conspicuous against the skeletons of new buildings, vacant lots, a parliament of idlers on the boulevard, weary laborers on bicycles, a Hebrew policeman in Bermuda shorts directing traffic on Allenby Street, a campfire built by Socialist youth, their voices raised in song: Tear down the old, herald the new. No aspect of the festivities was likely to arouse longing for the old world that was crumbling. The desperate attempt to construct a new ruin, a palace on sand, was touching and beautiful, but also baffling. The dancers moved less like figures tired of dancing than like people unable to discern whether the unfolding events were scenes in a movie, whether stagehands would appear to move the set, leaving a vacuum in space, a void filled with planks and backdrops, a spark extinguished before it was lit, arousing in Aminadav a sensation of challenge, of obstinate glory, of people who never submit, who persist, even behind prison walls, in enacting their own glorious opera.

21

Seven days of oppressive heat. A wind blew in from the desert, heavy and dry. People enclosed themselves in their houses, locking the doors and windows. Cars simmered in the streets. Trees were covered with yellow dust. The sky was clear and stiff as steel. The nights were cold. It looked as if one could walk the Milky Way. Aunt Shlomzion shut herself into the *hamsin* chamber for seven days. She didn't listen to the radio or read. She drank cold lemon juice and thought of the abandoned yard. She saw mad cats and had occasional fantasies in which gentlemen and ladies came out of the grand house to play tennis in the well-groomed yard. But they were no longer there. Secretaries in short dresses were typing letters in triplicate in air-conditioned rooms, addressed to nonexistent customers. The young lawyers appeared to be exhausted. The house was surrounded by shrubs that grew wild, dried-out grass and dead vines. Shlomzion was expecting Arty Brand and his family. It was three years since Nehemiah's death. In the morning Little Mother Shlomzion had called on the phone, and Shlomzion the Great had said we could come whenever we like, if we like; then she slammed down the receiver.

The following afternoon, two hours after Art's arrival, Mother called me. Art wants us to come immediately, she said. He arrived two hours ago. He says the heat is awful. He is in the house with Shlomzion and is very eager to see the family. He plans to stay two weeks.

Three weeks, Mother had corrected.

I decided to make it two weeks, he had said wearily, beginning to stammer.

We arrived at three. Arty Brand, his wife, Sandra, their oldest daughter and the twins sat in the cool shady *hamsin* room. Melissanda had stayed in the States. When we arrived, Arty whispered that they were only staying two days; they were going back, he explained shamefacedly, because something unexpected had come up. He had to get back.

It was hard to blame him.

The room seemed very crowded, with everyone seated in silence, focused on an imaginary center.

We hugged and kissed, exchanged polite emotional words, met the children. We kissed Shlomzion's powdered cheek, took our seats and were engulfed in hostile silence. The twins laughed and spoke English with a Midwestern accent. Sandra's eyes were filled with dry tears.

Shlomzion gazed into space and brushed my kiss off her powdered cheek, looking lovely against the play of shadows in the room. A picture of Nehemiah when he was a student in America hung on the wall. Shlomzion began to speak. She spoke to me. The room was filled with suppressed anxiety. Sandra stared at Art. Art stared at the floor. The twins giggled. Mother poured a cold drink. Aunt Shlomit brought the twins cookies, hoping to win their favor. But they were afraid of her. She was offended and sat knitting socks.

Shlomzion began talking. Was she talking to me?

My son, she said. How many years has he been gone? Fifteen, perhaps more. He came for a minute to see his father, then disappeared. He didn't come to the funeral. But he comes to my funeral. Today. He expects an inheritance. Is that why his mistress and his bastard children bothered to come? They don't even resemble our family. Whom do they resemble? Their Japanese father? Look at them. Adonsky's grandchildren. Listen: English only. He couldn't teach them a little Hebrew? Why? Come here, sweet twins. Iyy em your *savta!*

They pay no attention to her. The older one smiles. There is something defective about her, too. Shlomzion says: Come to Grandma. She might have something for you. They don't move; they just watch her. She sits like a master (Adonsky), like a deeply rooted oak, emitting hate, implanting enmity imbued with sweetness and cunning throughout the room. I am in love with you, old woman. She has always known the scent of a victim, and I am the victim of her subdued yet potent spell. She can trap me, but she cannot conquer, recognizing my values just because they don't apply to her.

She says: See his wife. See what he brings me. They are quiet. They just came and they're going already. Why? Our country isn't good enough? The heat, the *hamsin?* Is the weather better in Chicago? They have terrible blizzards in the winter and heat waves in the summer. Who doesn't know that. What do they want from me? You know, Ami, there was once a woman, a Mrs. K., who lived on Rehov Hayarkon. She had a four-room apartment, with three windows facing the sea. Not the anti-Semites' sea in Chicago, but the Jewish sea, here in Tel Aviv . . . She covered her walls with fabric. How do you say tapestries in Hebrew? We have no word. Too bad Dr. Bugrashov is dead. He had words for everything. I met Nehemiah in his house. Those were very intense times, full of hope. But not for Arpahshad and his wife or for the non-identical twins. Why aren't they at least identical? And wasn't Dizengoff trying to make out with me? You're surprised. They were all after me. Even in the days when I resisted Nehemiah's obstinate wish to steal my son from me. I was fighting for him. Now he is losing his hair. He's funny. He doesn't resemble me, Adonsky or Nehemiah. Maybe he's not really mine. He stammers. The first thing he did was look for the dog house. He may have thought I live there now. He's such an uncivilized person. Why doesn't he write to me? Why doesn't he love me? Why is he leaving when he just came? Huh? You tell me! . . . But that woman, Mrs. K., covered the walls with tapestries. Red ones with gold stripes. It was stunning. And, listen, she had plenty of money. It was her husband who sold your mother black-market meat for four years, all through the war. He sold to your mother and to several other innocent and humble ladies like your mother, who inherited her fine legs from her father. . . . Mrs. K. rented out rooms, though she had money and lots of it, while she herself—Ami, get this—she herself lived in the kitchen under the sink! It was appalling. I used to visit her and we would sit under the sink and talk about Adonsky's carriage or her first lover, a British officer killed by the stupid terrorists in Acre. She really lived under the sink, Ami.

Mother! . . . Art tried getting a word in, his voice seeming to rise out of a great abyss.

Listen, she said. I'm talking to Ami, who isn't running away from his mother. You know something: you'll never steal my rooms from me. I am a poor woman, unfortunate and lonely, but I have a few pennies collected from here and there, and I, Arpahshad, my dear, do not intend to live under the sink! . . . I will live here until my last day. It's my house, built by Adonsky. Nehemiah planted trees here. Listen, Ami, you are a violent person, but acceptable; reasonable, though not especially bright. Understand? Why are they like that? Look, they sit in silence. The children speak only English. Here, listen, children: Iyy em your *savta.* Iyy em geeving yu a prezent uff money. Heyr, twu grush! They don't come. They stare. What's the matter? My English isn't good enough for them? I'm not Mayflower like my son? I'm not from Japan like their mother? He married her. She can't even cook. She has a career? What for? What about her husband? What has she done to my son? Is this the child I struggled to bring up? Shattered and useless. Look at her! Look at her children. Are they hers? Maybe they're someone else's. Do the Japanese make children like white people do? . . . Did you know my son came on

the Mayflower? He's George Washington's direct descendant! Yess, tell me, tschildren, yuur fahzer iz frum Washington?
Mother.
Arpahshad.
My name is Art.
I'll tell you your name. You're not even converted. This is where you come from.
Mother.
Look at her, this creature from Japan: Madam Pototsky. What is she made of?
Mother.
Arpahshad.
Mother.
Ar—
Tomorrow we . . .
Arpahshad.
Mother.
M—

Art Brand and his family spent two days in the room. After which Sandra disclosed to Shlomzion what she had contained in her heart for fifteen years. She spoke and Shlomzion, like a true lady, didn't hear. She didn't consider it appropriate for her to listen to a Japanese whore who had utterly deceived her foolish son.

After Sandra concluded her monologue, Art stammered a few words, collected his family and went out to the street, which was still in the grip of the hot wind. He ran to the El Al office, made the necessary arrangements and, after three days, as if fleeing from fire, flew back to Chicago with his family. Aunt Shlomzion the Great claims that Little Mother Shlomzion convinced Art to leave early because she wanted my sister Hamutal either to marry him or to become his mistress so she would get in on the inheritance. She says that Mother, Hamutal and I will get a fig! Arpahshad will also get a fig! He can have the house, she said, as indicated in four out of her five wills, but only under the following conditions:

That his eldest daughter write her a letter stating that in her heart and soul she is Jewish and that she did not convert through her father's influence.

That Art change his name and revert to the one given him at birth.

That Sandra move out.

That his oldest daughter not marry a Christian or a black man.

That Art stop slandering Israel.

That each member of his family write her a letter in Hebrew apologizing for what was done to her.

I wrote to Art. He stammered a reply to me filled with panic and weary humor, stating that his daughter was living with a young man, not a Jew, and that she doesn't consider herself Jewish. Being a modern woman and a university graduate, she has no interest in Shlomzion's house. She would not write her a letter. Nor would he write. The twins do not know any Hebrew. So much for that.

The notion that Little Mother Shlomzion would want Hamutal, who has been married to a charming fellow for more than ten years, to marry her cousin for the sake of providing her, Little Mother Shlomzion, with some trifle from the old house of Shlomzion the Great—tattered, arresting, enormous and crumbling—evoked a cry from Mother such as I had heard only when Father died.

22

The years pass. Arty Brand arrived in the country last week. Mother wrote to him several times and he finally agreed to come.

Shlomzion's mind was deteriorating. She was losing contact with reality. She spent the day in bed, sobbing, hours on end, saying *tsif-tsif* to the birds.

She's full of birds now, Mother wrote.

Art arrived. He looked different. He has a young wife now. Sandra lives with another man in Massachusetts. His oldest daughter is about to be married. His wife and his daughter are the same age. He looks more thoughtful and innocent, elicits affection, pardon, bewilderment. He came to take leave of his mother. She will live one more day or perhaps another twenty years. Her body is not dead. She has become neither weak nor faint. Her hair is full. She is very beautiful. To this day she remains the most beautiful woman I have ever seen. But her mind is rapidly losing every link with reality. She complains that we steal books from her, writing paper, pencils, air.

She is consumed with hate but so senile that even her malice is incoherent. Something in her eyes is extinguished. She is enveloped in anguish, transparent and silken. There are moments when she looks like the child she could have been. She lives in another world. We don't know, as we could never know, what world she lives in.

Art brought his mother a gilded cage with a parakeet, which he hung over her bed. The nurses laughed, but not the doctor. He no longer performs those extra examinations. Mother is responsible for that. He hates her with a deadly passion and has turned his back on Art as well.

Old Judge Abrams died this week. We went to his funeral. The key to my aunt's financial maze was lost with him. Art will have to unravel the tangles. He sat with five lawyers, who pulled at their few remaining hairs. No one knows where to begin.

Abrams's funeral was attended by Little Mother Shlomzion, Hamutal, my wife and children, old Nahumi and me. A cantor sang the traditional prayers. Someone suggested that I say *kaddish*. They said I was a relative.

I said *kaddish* for him.

I was descended from the flowers he dried, the criminals he condemned to prison; kin to evil and beauty. In this manner I was betrothed again and again to Aunt Shlomzion the Great, so beautiful and so evil.

In the private hospital in north Tel Aviv the rates went up. The fee is now fourteen thousand lirot a month, owing to devaluation and other factors. Art hung the cage over Shlomzion's bed. There is a parakeet in it. The parakeet doesn't speak. He chirps.

She lies in bed all day, saying: *tsif-tsif, tsif-tsif.*

She will lie there many more days—years, perhaps centuries.

The parakeet will die; another will replace him. Someone will attend to the payments. Nahumi will soon die. He looks so bad that it would have made sense to embalm him at Abrams's funeral. They're all dying on me. Shlomzion's houses are growing rusty. Everything is sad, so sad. Art is gone. I stand in the hospital lobby. Amihud Milwite was here to find out if . . . I told him it was a matter of five to twenty years. He fled, poor fellow.

She lies there, a devastated palace, God in ruins, the shells flashing through her hair concluding a millennium. She remains a mountain of earth, humanity, evil and beauty. Pure as simulated crystal, she floats through an infinity filled with birds, despair and glory, chirping all the while: *tsif-tsif, tsif-tsif-tsif.*